WEAVING IS FOR ANYONE

Jean Wilson

Reinhold Publishing Corporation/New York
A Subsidiary of Chapman-Reinhold, Inc.
Studio Vista/London

To Jakie (1883-1966) — who reached his Finis before I did.

© 1967, Reinhold Publishing Corporation
All rights reserved
Printed in the United States of America
Library of Congress Catalog Card Number: 66-24552
Published in the United States of America, 1967 by
Reinhold Publishing Corporation
A Subsidiary of Chapman-Reinhold, Inc.
430 Park Avenue, New York, New York 10022
and in Great Britain, 1967 by
Studio Vista Limited, Blue Star House,
Highgate Hill, London N 19
Type set by Lettick Typografic, Inc.
Printed by New York Lithographing Corporation
Color Printed by Litholine Enterprises, Inc.
Bound by William Marley Company

All drawings are by Virginia von Phul.
All photographs, unless otherwise credited,
are by William Eng.

Foreword

In almost every culture in the world, a method of weaving has sooner or later been devised. The earliest weavings in cold climates were no doubt inspired by animal skins or pelts. Tropical peoples wove grasses and reeds for rain and wind protection — cool, lightweight garments and headgear.

Early potters used their woven baskets as molds to be packed with clay, which were then baked in the fire. Indians of the Northwest wove remarkably tight baskets to cook and store food in, and to carry water. Basket weaving techniques were transferred to flat weaving, to make blankets and mats. The fine linens and ramie cloth found in Egyptian tombs show a high degree of talent and skill in the weaving craft. Coptic tapestry; the awesome number of Peruvian weaving techniques; American Indian rug and blanket weaving; European and Asian tapestries and rugs — all over our world weavings have been found, and the many variations and methods passed along to us. Not too long ago a woolen mantle simulating the long pile of animal fur was found in Iceland; research placed the probable origin at about the year 1000. What a wealth of years, tradition, and experimentation is behind this weaving craft!

Cloth, dyes, spun and unspun fibers have been an important part of the world economy and trade since earliest times. Years ago, cloth was a very precious thing — especially to the American pioneers. The flax or cotton first had to be planted, tended, harvested, and prepared for spinning through many different steps. Then, finally, the threads were woven into fabric. The sheep and goats had to be tended and sheared; the wool cleaned, carded, and spun. It is no wonder that clothing, household linens, and coverlets were treasured, handed down in families, and used as long as threads hung together. Each yard of cloth represented untold hours of patient labor. The final disposition of the threadbare suit or bed curtains was to cut them into strips. These were carefully sorted, dyed, and woven into rag rugs.

Today, perhaps as a kind of protest to the busy, mechanized, and regulated world that we live in, people of all ages and interests are turning to handicrafts. We weave not so much from the necessity of making cloth to cover us or to beautify our surroundings, as from the human need to create something from raw materials. Weaving becomes an esthetic exercise, instead of a domestic chore. This, then, is a reason why we can try new effects. Our imaginations can soar — we can create something not necessarily useful. For the practical souls, something useful *and* beautiful, something individual, or one-of-a-kind can be made.

Begin your weaving with little outlay of money and time, and use some form of frame or box loom. We shall take you through several projects using different types of simple looms. Then, if weaving is really for you, go on to bigger and better weaving on a floor or table loom.

ACKNOWLEDGEMENTS

I am beholden to so many people for help and encouragement in putting this book together; when I listed their names, I knew there would not be nearly enough space to include all of them. Each photograph credit line represents one or more helpful, cooperative, and interested persons.

My sincere thanks:

• to each of you who generously allowed me to use photographs of looms, weaving, and collected fabrics.

• to Virginia Isham Harvey, who, in her multiple role as Preparator, Costume and Textile Study Collection, School of Home Economics, University of Washington, friend, fellow weaver and writer, has given of her time and knowledge so generously.

• to my friends who tested weaving directions for me: Marty and Cristy Owen, Kay McClinton, and Helen Tonning. And to all of you who were sounding boards for ideas.

• to my valued friend, Mary Hanson, who tested directions and went on to weave the pointing-hand tapestry; who has been a never-ending source of information, and who is always ready to play catch with ideas.

• to Virginia von Phul, who so expertly drew the diagrams showing you how-to-do-it, for her unstinted help, far beyond that of a good friend, in getting the manuscript ready and off to the publisher.

• to William Eng, whose excellent photography is such an important part of this book.

• to Jacqueline Enthoven, whose enthusiasm, gentle prodding, and good advice has been so helpful from start to finish.

• to The Seattle Weavers' Guild, for the continuing years of challenging programs, and for drafting me into doing workshop and study programs, with the privilege of working with stimulating and talented craftswomen, especially the Tapestry group.

• and most of all, I am grateful and warmed by the abiding patience and sustained interest of my family: my husband, Ron, who with his gentle teaching and awareness of design and the beauty in the world, has made me aware and appreciative; our son, Gary; and my parents, Jake and Belle Verseput, all of whom at times had to take second place.

Weaving is for anyone, and with so much interest, encouragement, and help, I now believe everyone is for weaving!

Jean Wilson
Bellevue, Washington
March, 1967

TABLE OF CONTENTS

Introduction

Because weaving *is* for anyone, our hope is that this book will provide ideas, inspiration, and techniques for everyone interested in this art: from a small child learning just how fabric is made by weaving over and under a warp, or a fond grandmother or young sister weaving a bib for the new baby; to an experienced weaver needing a way to do some quick sampling for color and texture, or to someone who has longed to make a tapestry — but has no loom. Perhaps we shall just help you to appreciate looking at tapestries and hand weaving.

We explore a very wide range of what to weave on and ways to weave, but still there are more. Detailed directions have been given where we thought they would be useful, especially for new weavers. All of the examples were carefully chosen to illustrate a point, but we consider each one to be an example of good design, choice of material, and technique. We hope that everyone will read the whole book, then go back to some special section that would be suitable for his or her talents and purposes. Our theme and theory are that anyone can weave on almost anything.

This book is for experienced weavers, who must do a great deal of sampling and experimenting. The author believes that the only true way to learn exactly what happens to colors in yarns of different weights, textures, lusters, spacings, crossings, and juxtapositions is to sample, sample, and sample again!

Of course, before doing a number of yards, you will want to sample the exact tie-up and sett on the loom you plan to use. With a quickly assembled frame or cardboard loom you can get a close approximation of a weave without having to use your large loom. Sampling on these small looms is also valuable to help estimate take-up and shrinkage. You can wash a little sample and get a fair idea of the amount of shrinkage. The sample can be stretched and pulled, steam pressed, and tested for color fastness.

Small cardboard looms and frames will allow you to do tapestries and still keep your floor looms free for other weaving that can only be done on a more complex loom. Also, these little looms and frames are necessary tools for experienced weavers of yardage, rugs, clothing fabrics, or upholstery. Color studies with paints can be made for a weaving project, but you still cannot find out what happens until the threads are brought together and interlaced. Even thorough color studies must be amplified and confirmed by actual samplings. For books on advanced as well as simplified weaving, see the Bibliography.

This book is also for young weavers. Handwork is unsurpassed as a method of showing children just how fundamental processes are performed. A valuable learning experience, it gives a better understanding of how things go together, and stimulates further search and reading. It may provide a lifelong interest, career, or hobby.

An activity well worth doing is making something useful, while employing design and color. Everyone should have an opportunity to learn how to use various materials, to get the feel of them in the fingers, to think through and create a design. A great deal of pleasure and satisfaction is to be had through constructing something out of the raw material. We learn through our hands. Start with a ball of yarn and transform it into a rug; gather an armful of reeds and weave them into a mat. Having produced a piece of weaving, you will forever have a greater understanding and interest in all fabrics. A new dimension of comprehension has been formed.

For you grandparents with some time to spare and a need to do something useful and creative, here is a craft made to order for you, your grandchildren, and young friends. Working through some of these weaving projects will be rewarding for all of you. A good many skills will be sharpened and discovered. Perhaps a grandfather will be of more help making a small loom, and grandmother can take over on the weaving; or all of you can become involved with a project from start to finish. Perhaps you will be able to take over a few craft sessions for a busy young den mother or scout leader. Brothers can make looms — and weave, too. Mothers and fathers will find rewards in helping children to learn a new craft. Father can work on loom building; Mother can advise on the weaving.

This book is for craft teachers who teach groups at any level of ability or age. Groups can do craft projects together. Children in summer camps, or in school classes in arts and crafts, Scouts, Campfire Girls, patients who need an interest and a new dexterity: all of these people benefit from working on weaving projects together.

The decorative bands used as embellishments in this book are finger weavings, Hungarian loom weavings, and Inkle loom weavings. (Adult student work. Courtesy of the Art Department, University of Washington. Richard M. Proctor, Instructor.)

1 The Language of Weavers

Weavers have their own distinctive and interesting vocabulary. With roots so far back in history, much symbolic analogy is found in poetry and prose. For example, "the web of life," "tangled web of deceit," "tissue of lies," "shuttling back and forth," "weaving in and out," have become common terms.

True craftsmen love the sound of their own special words. They come to mean special things, and it is always fun to have a secret vocabulary. A ripple of amused and understanding laughter ran around the table at a weavers' luncheon when a non-weaver guest heard one of the weavers confide to another that she had to move the lamms because she could not get a big enough shed. The guest questioned the weaver about her sheep raising and farm, and was abashed to learn that these lamms were part of the loom structure, and that helping to make a shed to put the shuttle through was their function!

The following definitions are limited to terms found in this text, and their meanings are given in relation to their usage in the book.

ILLUSTRATED DEFINITIONS OF WEAVING TERMS

ARC. Putting weft into shed in a curve, so that it will not be pulled too tight. This is also called "bubbling."

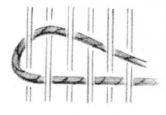

ARC

BACKSTRAP LOOM. This loom has one end of the warp fixed to a post or firm support; the other end attached to the weaver's waist. Also called girdle back, body, strap, or belt loom.

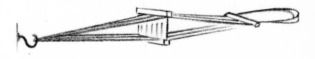

BACKSTRAP LOOM

BEAM. Bars at each end of loom to hold warp at the back, and cloth at the front.

BEATER, BEATER-IN. Device to push the weft down toward the cloth beam. Can be a comb, fork, block with nails, flat stick.

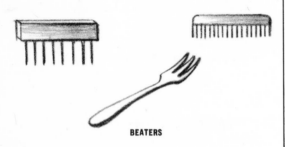

BEATERS

BOBBIN. A length of weft yarn wound around the fingers (see Butterfly), cardboard, shaped wooden shuttles, or a paper cylinder, which fits into a shuttle.

BOBBINS

BUBBLING. See Arc.

BUTTERFLY. A bobbin wound in a special way. See Chapter 6.

BUTTERFLY

CARTOON. Tapestry design drawn on paper.

CHANGE POINT. The place in tapestry weaving where one color leaves off and another color is started, in the same row.

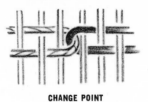

CHANGE POINT

CLOTH BEAM. Beam at the bottom or beginning of the warp, around which the woven cloth is turned.

COLOR BLANKET. A woven color study, where each color is woven over all colors. Sometimes called a "gamp."

CONTINUOUS WARP. In this text, a warp that is wound on the loom directly from the spool, without being premeasured.

CROSS. In this text, the crossing of the warp threads in a figure 8 warp.

CROSS

GAMP. See Color Blanket.

HEADING. A few rows of plain weave at the beginning of the weaving. Makes a straight row to begin weaving against; may be turned in for a hem on the finished fabric; helps to keep the main body of weaving from ravelling out when the warp is cut.

HEDDLE BAR, HEDDLE ROD, OR STICK. Holder for heddles.

HEDDLE BAR

HEDDLES. String loops to raise and lower warp threads when they are threaded through them.

HOLE AND SLOT HEDDLE. A rigid board with alternate holes and slots through which the warp threads are strung. It raises and lowers the alternate threads. Used on a backstrap loom.

HOLE AND SLOT HEDDLE

INTERLOCK. In tapestry weaving, where two colors in the same row of weaving meet, join, and return.

INTERLOOP. Method of joining two colors in Swedish knot tapestry.

LEASE STICKS, RODS, WARP STICKS. See Warp Sticks.

LIMNING. Outlining of a design in tapestry. Identified particularly with Peruvian weaving.

LIMNING

LOOM. A weaving frame. A device on which you can stretch a warp under tension.

OUTLINING. See Limning.

PICK. One row of weft across the warp. Row, shot, throw.

PILE WEAVE. Knotted weft, ends clipped so that surface is furry. Can be left uncut, in loops.

PILE WEAVE (CUT)   **PILE WEAVE (UNCUT)**

PLAIN WEAVE. Weaving over and under, one row. Under and over the next row. Sometimes called "tabby."

ROW. One line of weft across the warp.

SELVAGE, SELVEDGE. Woven edge of cloth. Usually made stronger by putting two or three warp threads together at the outside edge. Some weaving has four selvages.

SETT. The number of warp threads in 1˝ inch.

SHED. The triangular space formed when alternate warp threads are raised or lowered.

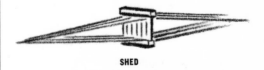

SHED

SHED STICK, SHED SWORD. Flat, smooth stick woven into the warp. When turned on edge, it makes a shed.

SHED STICK

SHUTTLE. Weft holder. Many different kinds for special purposes. Shown: boat, rug, stick.

SHUTTLES

TABBY. Plain Weave, with the same number of threads in warp and weft per inch. A perfectly balanced 50/50 weave.

TAKE-UP. The amount of warp used up through space taken by the weft. A consideration when weft is especially thick or big around, such as large rug yarn or round sticks and stems.

TAUT. Warp thread pulled and fastened so that there is no slack or sag.

TENSION. Warp thread tied fast at each end, to make it taut.

WAIST BEAM. In this text, the beam at the weaver's waist on a backstrap loom.

WARP. Threads stretched lengthwise on the loom, across which the weft is woven. The warp is the foundation of fabric.

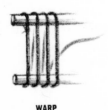

WARP

WARP BEAM. The beam at the back of a loom where the warp is tied.

WARP-FACED WEAVING. A fabric with the warp so closely spaced that the weft does not show.

WARP STICKS, LEASE STICKS, LEASE RODS, LAZE RODS. Sticks slipped in on each side of the warping cross, then tied together to keep the warp threads straight. Part of some primitive looms.

WARP STICK

WEAVING SWORD. See Shed Stick.

WEB. The cloth — finished weaving.

WEFT. The yarn that goes across the warp, making cloth.

WEFT

WEFT-FACED WEAVING. A fabric with the weft so closely packed or beaten in that the warp does not show, as in tapestry.

WOOF. Old-time term for weft.

2 Looms

What *is* weaving? There is really nothing very complicated about weaving. It is a logical process: you put a group of threads together, cross them with other threads, and then you have cloth. If you have a way of putting tension on a group of yarns, you can weave whether you have a real loom or not. Warp threads are the skeleton — the framework — the bones of the fabric. Weft threads cross the warp threads in variations of over one, under one, to create cloth.

First you need to have warp threads long enough to make your proposed fabric, whether 12 inches for a mat or 30 yards for draperies. Your loom becomes more complex as the warp is lengthened and the width increased. A rug or tapestry is a finished, complete unit when it is taken from the loom. It can readily and comfortably be done on a loom the size of the unit, without provision for rolling a large warp around a beam for continuing length.

On a narrow piece of weaving, you can easily run the weft in, over and under, with a small shuttle, needle, or bobbin. When a wide width is desired, it becomes more feasible to raise alternate warp threads all at once, making a shed, so that a shuttle of weft can be put through. Designs and pattern repeats can be put in with a needle, shuttle, or bobbin of contrasting yarn. For yards of patterned fabric, the design pattern must be threaded through many heddles. Then your loom is multiple-harness; i.e., it has successive rows of heddles, tied to treadles, so that the sheds are foot-controlled and the weaver can throw a shuttle the width of the warp and weave a whole row of pattern at once.

Necessary and productive as a many-heddled loom is, there is something basic and satisfying about covering each warp thread by hand, in a tapestry or needle technique. This satisfaction seems to be proved by the enormous interest in tapestry weaving and stitchery. Whatever the technique, as a weaver, you are offered almost limitless possibilities — depending, of course, on your enthusiasm and ambition!

LOOM CHARACTERISTICS

The amazing thing about the contrast between a very primitive loom and a huge mechanized power loom in a textile factory, is not the difference — but the similarity. Essentially, both looms have a stretched warp, a method for making a shed, a shuttle of some kind to carry the weft thread across the warp, and a beater to press the weft down, to make a fabric. Some of the simple looms we present here are fun to make and use, just as an experiment. Some of them will become favorite tools to use over and over again.

CARDBOARD LOOMS

Cardboard — useful, suitable, usually at hand in many sizes and weights — is a very good material for making small looms quickly at no cost. Keep a lookout for firm pieces of it in boxes, cartons, or backs of tablets. In this era of boxing and wrapping every product, you will be sure to find some cardboard that is usable. If not, use poster board or Bristol board.

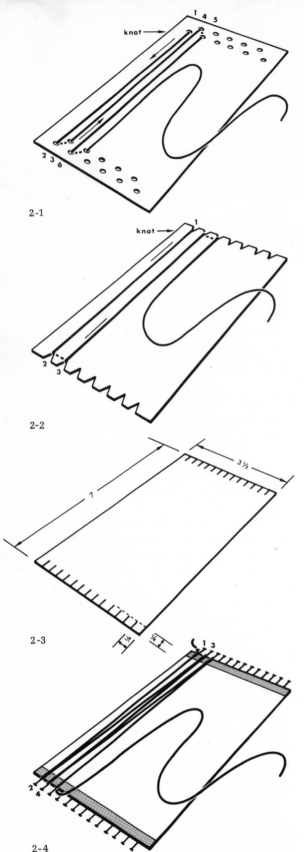

2-1

2-2

2-3

2-4

Flat cardboard looms

Here are four methods of making a flat cardboard loom, with a choice of ways to fasten and space the warp. You may prefer to cut notches or slits; or if your cardboard is very heavy and difficult to cut, it will be much easier to push ordinary straight pins in along each edge. A very young weaver might find the warp easier to handle if it is put through holes in the cardboard. The warp is then threaded into a large needle, and actually sewn to the loom. Holes can be made with a punch, or by pounding a nail into each mark for the warp.

FIGURES 2-1, 2, 3, 4. Four ways to fasten the warp on a flat cardboard loom. 2-1, Holes — staggered rows so that cardboard will have more strength. 2-2, Notches cut in. 2-3, Slits. 2-4, Common pins pushed into the thickness of cardboard. The tape across ends acts like binding to strengthen both sides.

Cardboard crescent loom

It is said that there is nothing new in the world, but the idea for this gently curved cardboard loom burst upon me as an "original." While warping a flat cardboard loom, I thought of slightly bowing it, to give working space under the warp. I named it "Crescent," and successfully and easily wove a small tapestry on it. A plain-weave tapestry is the project suggested for this loom, and directions for the loom and weaving will be found in Chapter 8.

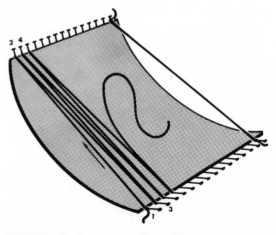

FIGURE 2-5. Crescent cardboard loom.

Flat circle looms

For a change and a challenge, try some weaving on a round flat loom. So many useful things can be made in this shape: coasters, hot-dish pads, place mats, sit-upon mats for floor or chairs, small rugs or pillows. The small items can be woven on a cardboard circle (2-8). The larger pieces can be done on a wheel-rim loom, and we have an idea for a round pillow that requires no loom at all (2-6, 2-7)! You will find directions for making and using these looms in Chapter 8.

Flat cardboard circle looms

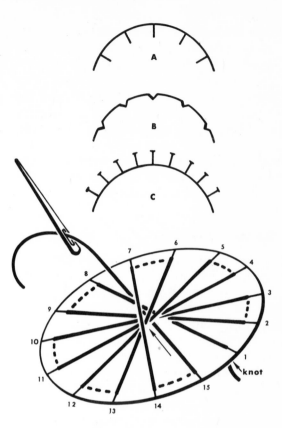

FIGURE 2-6. Wheel rim or hoop loom. (Courtesy of Interlake Manor, Bellevue, Washington.)

FIGURE 2-8. Flat cardboard circle loom. Three ways to hold the warp: slits, notches, pins.

FIGURE 2-7. Rag rug on wheel rim loom. Pillow woven over foam pillow form by author. (Wheel loom, courtesy of Interlake Manor, Bellevue, Washington; rag rug woven by a patient.)

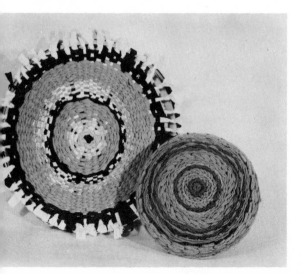

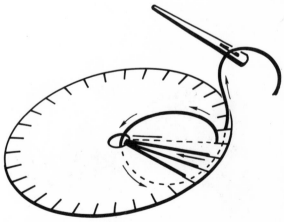

FIGURE 2-9. Flat cardboard circle loom with a hole in the middle, used to make reversible, double mats.

FRAME LOOMS

Picture frame looms

Ready-made picture frames are available in an unlimited number of sizes, kinds of wood, and widths. Getting one suitable for your purpose should be no problem. Perhaps you can find a used one around the house. Just be sure that it is clean, smooth, and squared-up with well-reinforced corners. Since the warp exerts a tremendous pull, the frame must be very firm and strong. Your weaving could become a disaster if the frame breaks or is racked out of shape.

Stretcher frame looms

Canvas stretcher frames, used by artists to hold their stretched canvas, are a real boon to weavers who want a quickly assembled frame, with no carpentry involved (2-11). Recently, a group of weavers came to learn how to do a tapestry on a frame loom. When they saw the canvas stretcher frame they departed as a group for the artist supply store. In about an hour they came back — each with a different size frame. The warps were soon on, and all weavers were happily doing tapestry!

The frame sections are available in a great range of sizes, wherever artist supplies are sold. From about 6 inches up to 48 inches or more, they can be bought in pairs for any dimension you need. Make a square or a rectangle — long and narrow or wide and short — the choice is yours. The unfinished wood is shaped like a piece of molding, but the corners are ingeniously fashioned into a fin and slot arrangement. These slip together and are very strong and rigid. Small wooden wedges are provided to drive in for further tightness, although we found they were not necessary. Perhaps with repeated dismantling, the joints might loosen up so that these would be needed. Metal frame reinforcements can be put in the corners. When you have finished a weaving project, the frames can be taken apart and used again in any other combination.

Moldings and trim for looms

Hardware stores and building supply firms have an assortment of trims and moldings, some of which are suitable for frames. These must be mitered at the corners, joined, and reinforced. Also, pairs of moldings for picture frames are available with the corners already mitered. They can be purchased like the stretcher frames, in pairs, to make almost any dimension. These are of sound wood, smoothly finished — a good choice if you do a picture weaving that should be hung with warp tension on. "Eucalyptus," Figure 4-6, an open-warp tapestry, was left on the weaving frame.

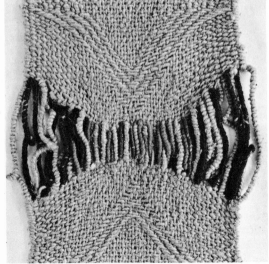

FIGURE 2-10. Wrapped weave, woven on a small frame loom. 6 by 14 inches. Silk and wool. (Courtesy of Sheila Hicks.)

FIGURE C-3. PERUVIAN MOTIF. Plain weave tapestry. Woven by the author. (Photograph by Dudley, Hardin, and Yang.)

FIGURE C-4. WATER BIRDS. Plain weave tapestry. Woven by the author. (Photograph by Dudley, Hardin, and Yang.)

FIGURE C-5. WATER BIRDS. Swedish knot tapestry. Woven by the author. (Photograph by Dudley, Hardin, and Yang.)

FIGURE C-2. NATIVITY. Swedish knot tapestry technique. Adapted from Christmas card sketch by Felix Campanella, Architect. Woven by the author. (Photograph by Dudley, Hardin, and Yang.)

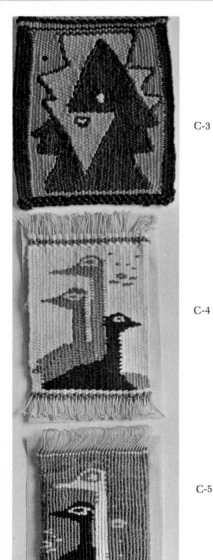

C-3

C-4

C-5

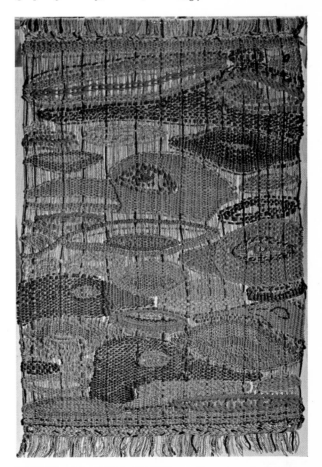

FIGURE C-6. BIRD HEADS. Tapestry techniques, needle stitches, and open warp wall hanging. Woven by the author. (Photograph by Dudley, Hardin, and Yang.)

How to make a raised beam loom

There is more than one way to utilize a frame as a loom. Here are several ideas, and you will probably devise a few more to suit your particular purpose. You may find it easier to weave with the warp on a slant. To do this, we constructed a raised beam loom (we also call it our "quick" loom). A trip through a hardware store yielded all kinds of ideas for beamholders. The one that worked the best was assembled in just a few minutes, and can be dismantled just as fast. This loom is ideal for people with no tools or carpentering ability. Its cost was less than $3.00. It can be used over and over again, and it works!

You will need

Four sides of a canvas stretcher frame.
Two broom or tool holders with a screw built in.
A piece of dowel to fit into the holders.
If you want a completely raised warp (this is probably an even better idea), put another pair of holders and a dowel at the opposite end of the frame.

FIGURE 2-12. The quick loom assembled.

A ready-made frame loom

Lilette, a fine little 15 by 20 inch frame loom, manufactured by the Lily Mills Company, Shelby, North Carolina, includes everything you need, except the warp and weft, to start right off weaving (2-13). The enclosed directions are clearly written with photographs showing step-by-step how to do it. The cost is moderate, and the frame is of beautifully finished hardwood. We made the tapestry, "Trees," on a Lilette loom. See Figures 4-1 and C-1. A heavy gauge wire along each side helps even a new weaver to create a mat, guest towel, bath mat, or units of a rug or coverlet, with good straight selvages.

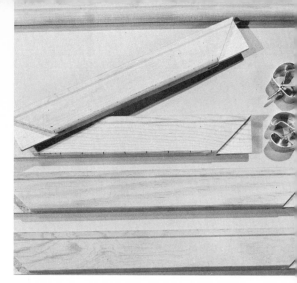

FIGURE 2-11. Frame loom parts for the quick loom. Four canvas stretcher frame sections, two broom holders, and one dowel.

FIGURE 2-13. Lilette Loom. Weaving sword makes a shed. Note heavy wire at each side to help weave straight edges. (Courtesy of the Lily Mills Company, Shelby, North Carolina.)

Looms with warp around the frame

Also, the warp can be wound around the frame either in a figure 8 (See Warping) or round and round. A continuous warp is used from the spool. A striped warp is wound and tied where each new color starts. See warp for gamp, Figure 5-1.

Another type of frame loom   Camden P.L.

On this frame loom, which has dowels for warp beams, all of the weaving is done inside and independent of the frame. The idea works well for a large size frame as well as for a small lap loom. Dowels should be about one-half an inch shorter than the inside measurement of the frame. Put a long bolt through the dowel and the frame, and fasten it with a wing nut at the outside edge of the frame. Either a figure 8 warp or a continuous round and round warp is satisfactory. String heddles can be installed.

If you wish, you can add holders for the heddle bar (2-15). The heddle bar is lifted, put into the notches, and is out of your way so that your hands can be free to put in the weft. To close the shed, lift out and lay the bar on the warp.

Frame looms with nails as warp holders

To weave a tapestry with the wrong side facing the weaver, a flat, even warp is made on rows of nails driven into the frame (2-16). Since all of the mechanics of weaving and warp fastening are hidden on the back of the frame, this method is especially good to use when you want your woven picture already framed. Cut the end of the last weft yarn, remove the stretching ties from along the sides, turn the frame over, and hang it on the wall!

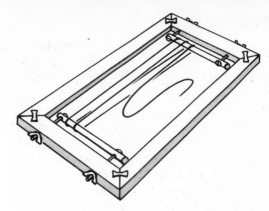

FIGURE 2-14. Frame loom, dowels added for warp beams.

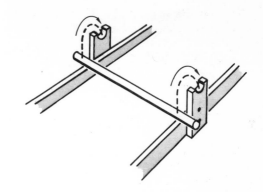

FIGURE 2-15. One way to add holders for the heddle bar.

FIGURE 2-16. Reverse side of canvas stretcher frame loom to show how nails may be put into frame top and bottom. The front of this Swedish knot tapestry is on page 135. (Courtesy of Sonia Ann Beasley.)

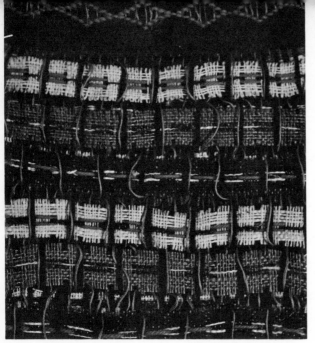

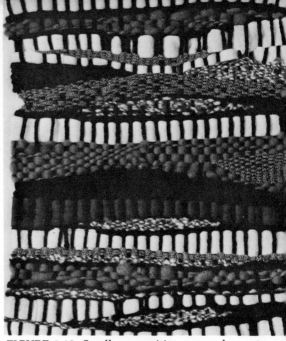

FIGURE 2-17. Mat woven on a simple board loom. Strips of burlap, cotton and linen yarns. Diamond design put in with a needle, over warp threads. (Courtesy of the Sammamish High School Art Class. Photograph by Clydene Phelps.)

FIGURE 2-18. Small composition woven by a student, on a board loom like the drawing shown in Figure 2-29. Study of materials and forms. Black wool warp, strips of white felt cut in contours, heavy olive-green wool, rayon, and flecked yarn in the same green. (Adult student work. Courtesy of the Art Department, University of Washington. Richard M. Proctor, Instructor.)

FIGURE 2-19. Wall hanging with warp an important part of the design. Gold and orange. Plain weave, areas of plain weave tapestry circled with jute. (Collection of Phil Hart. Mary Balzer Buskirk, weaver.)

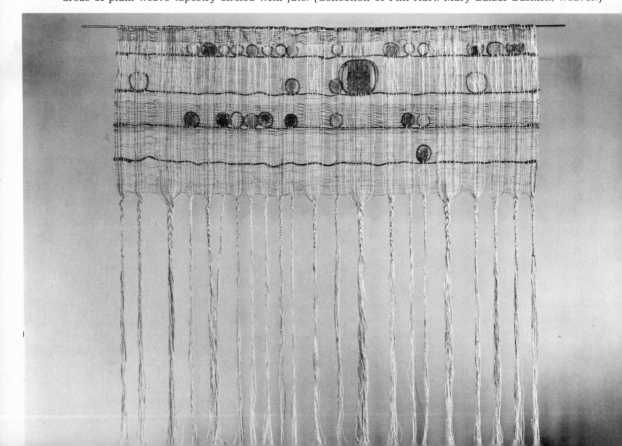

FIGURE 2-20. A simple weave, but lively and interesting because of the wefts used. The warp is heavy cotton rug yarn. Weft is of inside-peel bamboo strips, alternating with two strips of very fine matchstick bamboo, one natural and one dyed brown. (Courtesy of the Sammamish High School Art Class. Photograph by Clydene Phelps.)

FIGURE 2-21 . A rug like this can be made on a large, heavy frame with nails on all four sides — just a big edition of the little frame you might use for a small mat. Jute warp, flat weave between areas of pile. Ghiordes knot technique. Darker portions are composed of many shades of green and blue wool; large, lighter areas are a pencil-sized gray-green linen. Jute warp is green. Warp is braided at each end, all the warps in the flat weave strips are put into one fat braid. Woven by the author.

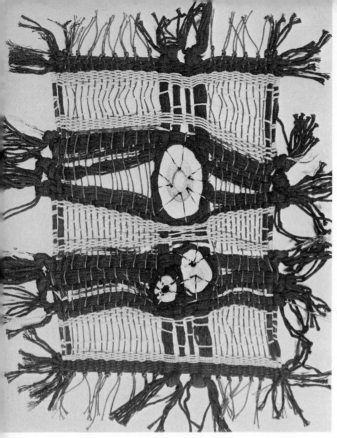

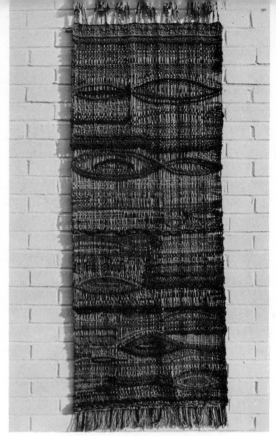

FIGURE 2-22. Open weave with inserts of ceramic shapes, pierced and fastened into the weaving with needle stitches. The weft extends beyond the selvage, is knotted like the warp ends for a fringe finish on all four sides. (Adult student work. Courtesy of the Art Department, University of Washington. Richard M. Proctor, Instructor.)

FIGURE 2-23. Open weave wall hanging. Warp of many colors and kinds of yarn, nubby and smooth, is part of the total design. Plain and tapestry weave, some needle stitches for emphasis of line and added texture. Bottom end finished in a Philippine edge, which looks like a braid but allows the warp to show as a straight fringe. Woven by the author. (Photograph by Don Normark.)

FIGURE 2-24. Place mat. Could be used with pottery dishes, perhaps on an outdoor table. Strips of folded cotton cloth, dried reeds, and heavy cotton yarn. Warp is the same cotton yarn.

Frames for rug looms and wall hangings

Large versions of this simple frame and nail loom are used to weave wall hangings and rugs. Here is a loom that should be tailored to the weaving. If you are going to weave a large, heavy rug, make your frame sturdy and strong, reinforced, and use large nails on all four sides. This will insure a good, square result. For a lightweight, open-weave wall hanging, perhaps with stiff wefts of reeds or some such material inserted, a lighter frame is suitable, with nails along the top and bottom only. Our drawing is just a point of departure. Make your frame and nail loom to suit your project.

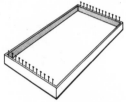

FIGURE 2-25. Simple frame loom with nails. Can be built in a large size for weaving units of rugs or whole rugs. Use heavier wood, reinforce corners, big nails.

FIGURE 2-26 Lightweight, portable frame, 48 inches by 18 inches. Weave rugs, tapestries, wall hangings; or units of blankets or rugs — to be joined together. (Courtesy of Craftools, Inc., Wood-Ridge, New Jersey.)

Variation on a frame loom

A high school senior learning to weave, and her father, devised this frame loom. By the addition of a U-shaped frame which swings up, and a double row of nails to hold the warp, a shed is made. A frame of this type, in a larger size, would be an excellent loom for weaving rug units.

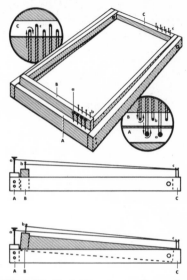

FIGURE 2-27. Variation on a frame loom. Shed device, with extra frame. (Courtesy of Allan and Clydene Phelps.)

FIGURE 2-28. Handbag of black and white wool, plain tapestry with hatching. Very firm — almost rug weight. Woven on the frame loom in Figure 2-27. (Courtesy of Clydene Phelps, weaver. Photograph by Clydene Phelps.)

BOARD LOOMS

A board loom is a much more substantial version of a flat cardboard loom. It is rigid, strong, and simple to make. All you need is a piece of plywood, two boards for end pieces — about $1/2$ inch to 2 inches thick — nailed or glued on, and nails pounded in across each end to hold the warp. The end pieces raise the warp enough for some working space underneath, and make it easier to put the shuttle through.

SHAPED BOARD LOOMS

If several pieces of weaving are to be made on a shaped loom, it is more satisfactory to make the loom from a piece of plywood, with nails, than from cardboard and pins. Each kind will work, but if a grandmother wants to weave many bibs, she will want to have a sturdier loom to use over and over. For more ideas on shaped weaving, see Figure 6-8.

HUNGARIAN LOOM

Hungarian weaving is a type of braid or strip weaving. The loom is a simple one, just a board with a bar at the end making a T shape, and nails on three sides. The directions for its use are easy to follow, but lengthy, and space does not permit including them. Our Bibliography notes where you can find two good sources of clear directions on how to do this weave. Hungarian weaving is fast, easy, and a way to weave long bands on a short loom. We hope you will investigate the possibilities. A few of the many patterns possible are shown in Figure 2-32.

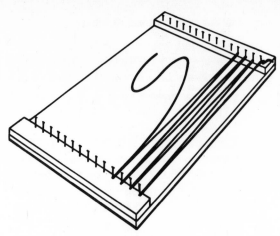

FIGURE 2-29. Simple board loom with raised ends.

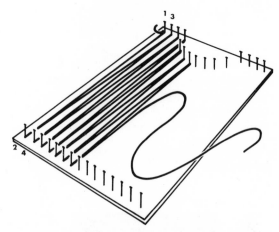

FIGURE 2-30. Shaped weaving on a board loom. Baby bib. The finished product and how-to-do-it are described in Chapter 8. Woven by the author.

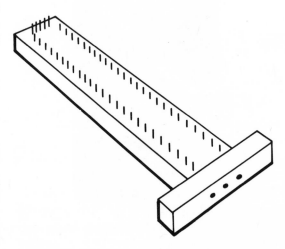

FIGURE 2-31. Hungarian loom — to make braid-like strips of weaving.

FIGURE 2-32. Hungarian weaving. The bands were woven on a Hungarian loom. (Adult student work. Courtesy of the Art Department, University of Washington. Richard M. Proctor, Instructor.)

ORIENTAL KNOT LOOM (TWO-WARP LOOM, TURKISH KNOT LOOM)

This two-warp loom is not quite a board loom — nor yet a box loom, but something of each. It is a very elementary loom, with a minimum number of parts (2-33). Detailed instructions on just how to make this loom are included with the rug weaving project in Chapter 8.

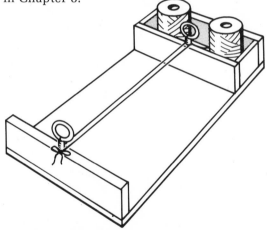

FIGURE 2-33. Oriental knot loom. Weave knots on two warps; sew fluffy knotted strips together for rugs.

How it works

A warp from each spool is fastened to the screw eyes, knots are made over the warps with cut lengths of yarn. The result is a strip of knotted cut pile. These strips are sewn together for a richly deep pile rug. These rugs qualify as strip weaving, scrap weaving, or rug weaving.

Advantages of using this simple loom and technique

Being light and portable, the loom can eas-ily be held on the lap or put on a table. As no great strength is required in the hands, and the units of weaving are not very bulky or heavy, it is an ideal craft for children, older people, and bed patients.

Design and color possibilities are almost unlimited, and a very rich, beautiful result is obtained with relatively small cost. In addition, odd lengths of leftover yarn can be used. Weavers always have boxes of thrums, which are the ends of warp left when weaving is cut from the loom. Several strands of a fine yarn, wool, cotton, and synthetic fiber can be used as one strand to make a very good-looking and long-wearing rug. This method of weaving is excellent "pickup" work; i.e., it can be put down and started again without difficulty or danger of mistakes.

BOX LOOMS

Box looms are easy to come by, and there are as many kinds as there are suitable boxes! Those especially favored for looms are the shallow wooden fruit or vegetable lugs, with nails pounded in along the edge of the two ends, much like our frame loom drawing. Deeper boxes are easier to use if the sides are cut down. Strong cardboard boxes can be used with pins or slits to hold the warp. A hosiery box, with both halves used, one inside of the other for strength, makes a good little loom with pins upright along the ends. Some boxes grow into regular table looms, with dowels for warp and cloth beams. A rigid heddle is the beater and shed-maker.

VERTICAL LOOMS

Upright or vertical looms, in use since very early times, range from the first warp-weighted looms suspended from a tree branch, and the familiar Penelope loom on a Greek vase, through all the versions of Indian rug looms, A-frames, and square frames, to the enormous tapestry looms of France. These looms have warps suspended from huge beams, roller devices to permit moving the finished weaving out of the way, and hundreds of string heddles; but the basic principle is the same as for a small vertical tapestry loom used in the home.

FIGURE 2-35. Dryad Standard Loom, vertical rug loom. Rugs and tapestries up to 7 feet long and 32 inches wide can be woven on this loom. (Courtesy of Craftools, Inc., Wood-Ridge, New Jersey.)

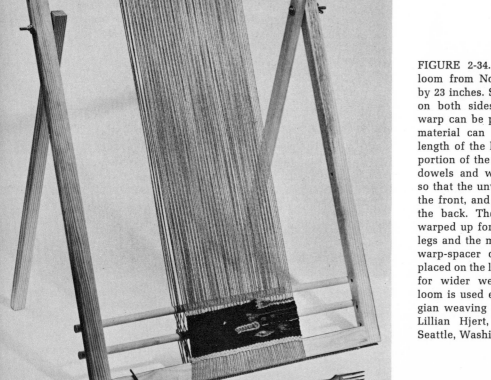

FIGURE 2-34. A vertical tapestry loom from Norway. Table size, 18 by 23 inches. Shown with one warp on both sides of the frame. The warp can be pulled around so that material can be woven twice the length of the loom. When the front portion of the warp is all filled, the dowels and warp are manipulated so that the unwoven warp comes to the front, and the woven part is at the back. The loom can also be warped up for just one length. The legs and the metal spring used as a warp-spacer can be removed and placed on the long sides of the frame for wider weaving. This type of loom is used extensively in Norwegian weaving schools. (Courtesy of Lillian Hjert, Magnolia Weaving, Seattle, Washington.)

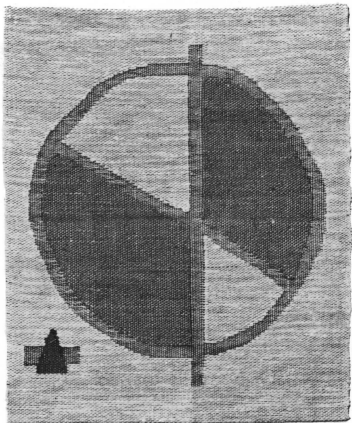

FIGURE 2-36. Small tapestries made in Norway, Sweden, and Finland. They were probably made on a loom similar to the Norwegian tapestry loom shown in Figure 2-34. (Courtesy of Lillian Hjert.)

BAG LOOM

"Ojibway," "free-warp," "bag," and "tubular weaving" are different names for a very simple loom, on which seamless tote or book bags are woven. The Ojibway and other Indians wove cornhusk carrying bags on this kind of vertical loom.

The loom consists of only four parts: top, bottom, and two dowels for the upright side pieces. At a cost of about $3.00 the Lily bag loom, which is smoothly finished hardwood, is a good buy (2-37). It arrives unassembled. All you do is put the dowel uprights into the holes on the top and bottom pieces. Since two sets of holes are provided, you have a choice of widths for your weaving.

FIGURE 2-37. Bag loom. Vertical loom. Weave from top down, to make shopping bags, carry-all bags. (Courtesy of the Lily Mills Company, Shelby, North Carolina.)

How to make a bag loom
You will need

> Two strips of wood about 15 inches long, 2 inches wide, and 1/2 inch thick.
> Two lengths of 3/4-inch dowel, about 18 inches long.

Rout or drill holes in the top and bottom pieces of wood, 12 to 15 inches apart, or whatever width you want to weave the bag. Fit the dowels into the top and bottom holes.

How to weave on a bag loom

Twining (7-20) is the traditional method of weaving on this kind of loom — the same technique used in weaving baskets. Quite a bit of variation and interest is possible, through rows of tightly packed warp contrasted with open warp rows. Use of colored stripes, or twining with two different colors is effective. The open, bottom end is knotted and fringed for a fancy finish. The bag can be turned inside out and knotted on the inside so that the bottom edge will be a plain seam on the outside. Handles can be incorporated as part of the warp. They will last longer than if they are sewed or knotted on later.

FIGURE 2-38. Method of warping the bag loom.

FIGURE 2-39. Bag woven on bag loom as it came off the loom. Woven by student in Grade 5. (Courtesy of Eleanor Hegge.)

BACKSTRAP LOOMS

Body loom, girdle-back, waist, stick, or belt loom — all of these are basically the same, and all depend upon the weaver for warp tensioning. A one-woman, arm-span loom is a good definition. One end of the loom and warp is fastened to a post, hook, tree, doorknob, or anything that will withstand a steady pull. The other end, the weaving end of the loom, is fastened around the waist of the weaver. An arrangement of warp lifters — string heddles or a rigid hole and slot heddle — control one shed; a sword or shed stick controls the alternate shed. Backstrap looms, employed during the very early days of weaving, are still in use all around the world. Weavers in the Asian countries, Scandinavia, Lapland, South America, Mexico, and Guatemala weave on these looms which have not changed much from the early primitive looms.

In our Project section, we have given you complete instructions on how to weave on a backstrap loom. Photographs show several kinds of backstrap looms and some fabrics that have been woven on them.

These looms are difficult to learn on, because the weaver is so much a part of the equipment. It takes a little maneuvering to maintain an even tension on the warp while you are controlling the heddles, putting in the weft, beating it down, and then trying to reach those scissors which are usually an exasperating 5 feet away! However, it is fun, and you do have a good feeling of being in control of the whole process. Study the complicated pattern weaves from Guatemala and Peru — the intricate, beautiful bands done by the Lapps. Do not be discouraged; simple weaving is lovely, too. Just remember that each of these things was done by just one person, with an arm-span about the same as yours. Try it!

FIGURE 2-40. Backstrap loom, Hawaiian version. Continuous raffia warp on two dowel rods for warp and cloth beams. (Courtesy of Jean J. Williams. Photograph by Thelma Warner.)

Hawaiian backstrap loom

On the Hawaiian version of a backstrap loom (2-40), the warp is spaced with a chained binding thread close to the rods. One shed is made with a dowel for a heddle stick. Linen thread heddles are looped around the dowel and every other warp thread in a figure 8. The second shed is made by slipping a cardboard tube under the alternate warp threads, to serve as a lifter. A length of threads is run through the tube and tied over the top of the warp. This represents the hollow log used in this position by primitive weavers. This loom is similar to backstrap, waist, or girdle looms used the world over. Although they vary in detail — such as what material is used for heddles, how heddles are attached, whether lease sticks are used, and what is used for a beater — basically they all follow the same plan.

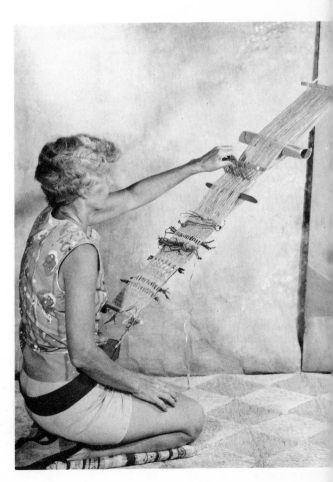

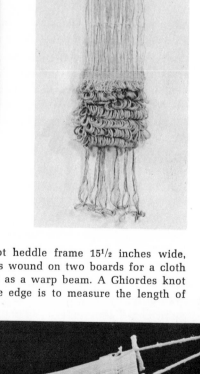

FIGURE 2-41. A small backstrap loom from the village of Magdalenas, Chiapas, Mexico. Overall size is 12 by 20 inches. Weaving: inset for huipil (blouse or dress), 6 by 10 inches. From La Tienda, Seattle, Washington. Collection of the author.

FIGURE 2-42. Backstrap loom, Norwegian version. Hole and slot heddle frame 15½ inches wide, spaced so that warp will be eight to the inch. Finished weaving is wound on two boards for a cloth beam. Note that warp or lease sticks are used at the opposite end as a warp beam. A Ghiordes knot pile fabric for a pillow is being woven. The white tape along the edge is to measure the length of the fabric to be made. (Courtesy of Gladys McIlveen.)

FIGURE 2-43. THIS IS A PEOPLE STOPPER. So named by the weaver who makes them. A product of our day of large expanses of glass windows and sliding doors. This is a weaver's answer to the problem of warning people that "this is glass, don't walk through!" About 6 inches wide, it is a perfect project for a backstrap loom. Shades of orange, gold, and deep pink in varieties of sisal, linen, cotton, wool, and nubby yarn. Open warp, tied or not, leno and loops all add interest. It would be just as effective hung on a wall as a gay shaft of color. (Courtesy of the weaver, Luana Sever.)

Mexican backstrap loom

The material in Figure 2-41 was woven on a small backstrap loom from the isolated village of Magdalenas, in the highlands of Chiapas, Mexico. The warp and cloth beams of the loom are lengths of a very hard stick-like reed. Heddle-rod, shuttle, and weaving sword are all small, peeled sticks. The warp is lashed to the top and bottom beams of the loom, with a twisted cord. A stretcher, inserted on the reverse side to keep the fabric an even width, is made of an unpeeled, straight, hard reed. A thorn nearly 2 inches long, in the hollow end of the reed, is used like a pin and put through the selvage. Ends of the thorn can be seen where the stretcher is placed, beside the small figures at the top of the weaving. Heddles are made by looping a thread around every other warp, then up and over the heddle stick. The overall size of the loom is only 12 by 20 inches. The woven piece measures 6 by 10 inches.

The warp is very fine, but rough cotton. The design is of handspun wool in brilliant shades of red, orange, turquoise, hot pink, and saffron yellow. The white plain-weave background around the little figures is the same fine cotton as the warp. The size and shape of the weaving would indicate that this was intended for part of the patterned insets which compose the sleeve of the full-length or blouse-length huipil, woven and worn by the women of the Tzotzil group, who live in Magdalenas.

Norwegian backstrap loom

In Figure 2-44, the weft of gray wool worsted is a closely beaten plain weave to cover the warp of white cotton. Stripes of black, lighter gray, and olive green were added with a needle while the fabric was still on the loom. The bag is made of strips woven in two different widths. Enough was made for the bag, then the loom was warped for a long, long strip of narrow wool for the handle. One continuous length forms the sides of the bag and the shoulder strap. Nice details of finishing are noted: warp ends of the strap are left as a 1-inch fringe where they join the bottom of the bag. The top edge of the bag is not hemmed, but the warp ends are double knotted and trimmed very short. The fastener is a crocheted loop of gray wool, over a handmade silver button. Pillow seams and bag seams are blanket stitched in the same gray wool. We think that these are good examples of thoughtful, complete design right for the loom used, finished with care and suitability.

FIGURE 2-44. Shoulder-strap bag and pillow, both woven on the Norwegian backstrap loom. (Courtesy of Gladys McIlveen.)

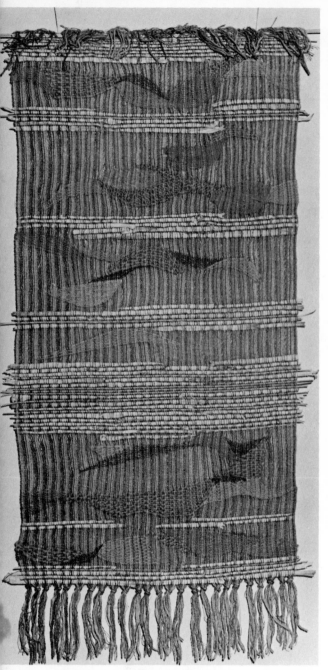

FIGURE 2-45 Wall hanging of linen, dried corn-husks, and vegetable-dyed wool. Flowing, twisting forms float in and out of the cornhusk stripes. (Collection of Diane Williams. Mary Balzer Buskirk, weaver.)

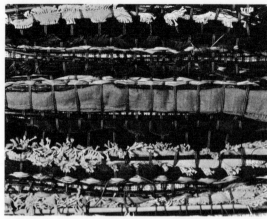

FIGURE 2-46. Experiment in materials and textures. Strips of cloth hemmed or frayed, on a cotton warp. (Courtesy of the Sammamish High School Art Class. Photograph by Clydene Phelps.)

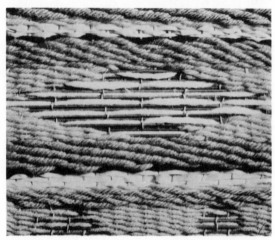

FIGURE 2-47. Mat of cotton rug yarn, fine bamboo and flat grasses. (Courtesy of the Sammamish High School Art Class.   Photograph by Clydene Phelps.)

TD loom

Probably every little summer-camper or craft group member has become acquainted with the TD loom — "TD" for Tongue Depressor. It is a quick, inexpensive, and small version of a backstrap loom. The hole and slot heddle is made of TD's — one at the top, one at the bottom, stapled to a row of vertical TD's. Each strip, after a hole has been bored in it, is placed just far enough from the next strip to leave a slot. Good directions for making these looms are found in many craft books. See the Bibliography.

FIGURE 2-48. Shoulder bag used by men of Crete. Woven of black and white handspun wool on white cotton carpet warp. Tapestry technique. (Courtesy of Ruby W. Burkheimer. Photograph by Fortescue.)

FIGURE 2-49. Two extremes of fabric weight, both woven in the Philippines, where much weaving is accomplished on backstrap looms. The lovely sheer stole is woven of palest yellow piña cloth. The thread is spun from fiber of pineapple leaves. Stripes and design of thatched huts and coconut trees are laid in for a border. In contrast, the cotton striped yardage is crisp and firm, woven of very fine, closely set, tightly beaten cotton with a ridged surface. Colors are bold, with widest stripes of white and golden yellow; pattern stripes and outlines are black, deep green, and dark red. (Collection of the author.)

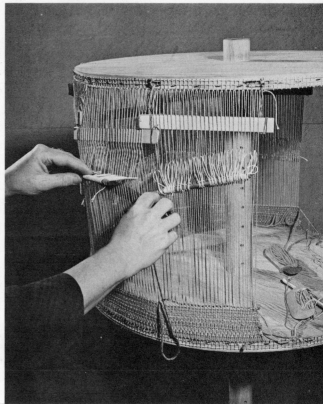

FIGURES 2-50, 51, 52. The round loom. Pilot model of round loom which is in the process of development. Much experimental work is still being done. Permanent models would be of fine woods and attractive materials. Shown warped for a wide, short, rectangular wall hanging. For tubular weaving, the warp is continued completely around the circle. (Courtesy of Virginia Isham Harvey.)

THE ROUND LOOM FOR TUBULAR WEAVING: A NEW PRINCIPLE IN LOOM DESIGN

Virginia Isham Harvey, a talented and experienced weaver, wanted to make a tubular piece of material with finished edges, to be attached to a leather top and bottom for a pouch bag. So she designed and constructed a loom to do just that! As she used the pilot model, she realized that there was a great potential in this kind of loom and weaving.

How it differs from other looms

It is possible to weave tubular fabric on a conventional loom, but it is not possible to weave it with selvage edges. On the round loom, rectangular or square flat fabrics with four selvage edges can be woven by warping a section of the circle and weaving first from left to right, and then from right to left. Part of a circle could be woven by using a smaller circle on the upper part of the loom. This would create a wedge shape, and would be woven back and forth like the rectangular shape. The round loom offers a good solution for a tapered lamp shade — or for mats to fit a round table.

How the round loom can be used

Tubular fabric is constructed by weaving round and round continuously, with the upper and lower circles the same size. The length of the tube depends upon the length of space between the circles. The diameter of the tube would depend upon the size of the circles. Each loom could be equipped with many pairs of circles.

FIGURE 2-52. Weave a tubular section for a bag with leather top and bottom; or a seamless drawstring bag. With a smaller circle at the top of the loom, a tapered tube can be woven.

Techniques

The model in Figure 2-50 will not produce a shed, nor does it have a beater. It is ideal for finger techniques such as soumak, tapestry weaves, and twining. String heddles can be installed to make one shed, as shown in the photographs. Since the round loom is warped directly from the spool, no premeasuring is necessary.

Advantages

Easy, relaxed weaving is possible on the round loom. The loom moves, and you sit still. Less space is needed for storage. It can be adjusted up and down, and has all the advantages of a tapestry loom, plus the tubular weaving possibilities. This loom can be made in a small, portable table model size with all of the same features as the larger floor model. It would work very well for bed- or wheel-chair patients, because it rotates to come to the weaver.

What you can weave on the round loom

The round loom is excellent for tubular materials for handbags, shaped garments, lamp shades, hats; for flat weaving, and segments of circles with all edges finished; for tapestries, place mats, rugs, and many other articles.

FIGURE 2-53. Silk and wool, wrapped and plain weave. (Courtesy of Sheila Hicks, weaver, and the Kunstgewerbemuseum, Zurich.)

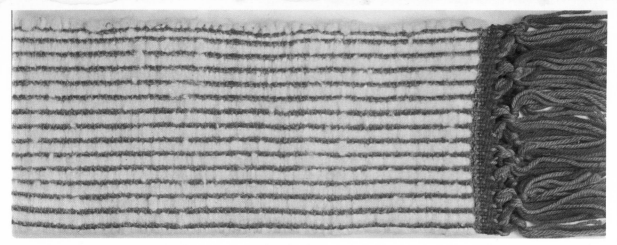

FIGURE C-7. Unspun white wool, cloud soft, thick as a finger. The orange stripes are wool warp. Woven by the author. (Photograph by Dudley, Hardin, and Yang.)

FIGURE C-8. Two color blankets. One is coarse wool, woven by the author. The other is very fine cotton. (Courtesy of Margery DeGarmo, weaver. Photograph by Dudley, Hardin, and Yang.)

FIGURE C-9. Collaborate with an artist, and weave from a painting. Traditionally, French tapestries are designed by artists, woven by expert craftsmen. (Courtesy of Edwin Danielsen, artist. Photograph by Ron Wilson.)

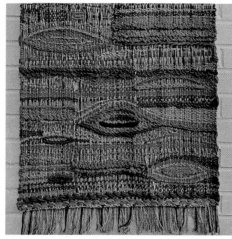

FIGURE C-10. Wall hanging showing tapestry techniques, loops, modeled wefts. Woven by the author. (Photograph by Don Normark.)

FIGURE C-11. CHILKAT BLANKET. Very old and very well done. Although age has faded the colors, pale yellows and blues can still be seen. (Courtesy of Gene Zema. Photograph by Don Normark.)

FIGURE 2-54. A warm, autumn-leaf brown, fine alpaca, woven in a reversed twill (pointed herringbone type), forms a diamond pattern in the body of this Mochica cloth. The border is plain weave with interlocked tapestry patterns. Black and brown birds, beaks open, tails up, and feet in running position, give an impression of great urgency. They seem to be hurrying off somewhere. The fringed edge is thick, and shows how many very fine warp threads are employed. (Courtesy of Dr. and Mrs. Palmer Beasley.)

WEAVING AND LOOMS FROM OTHER PLACES, OTHER PEOPLES, OTHER TIMES

Space permits only a brief mention of a few other weaving methods and looms — our heritage from weavers who went before. We urge you to investigate some of these techniques and devices through references in the Bibliography. You will find it a fascinating study. We are indebted to the crafts of many other cultures, and to the people of ancient times, for their practical as well as imaginative approach to weaving.

Legacy from master craftsmen

The legacy of weaving devices, design, and techniques from the master weavers of Peru is invaluable. A lifetime could be spent just studying and reconstructing their methods of weaving and textile decoration. American Indians, Mexicans, Guatemalans, Asians, Scandinavians, Lapps, Africans, Greeks, Egyptians, and many others — from all over this earth — have contributed inspiration and ingenious ways to construct fabrics on simple looms. Some of these fabrics are astonishingly sophisticated and finely done on crude equipment. Each culture, from its many small groups within, has contributed some new idea or a variation on an existing method to the craft of weaving.

Peru

The fascination of Peruvian weaving is compelling. It is almost impossible for a weaver to view these examples of the fabric arts casually, or to speak of them in anything but extravagant words. Skillfully spun fibers, as well as nearly every basic weave and method of fabric decoration, besides some techniques peculiarly Peruvian, present an exciting study.

Yarns used

The Peruvian weavers possess wool from alpaca, llamas, and vicuña. Cotton is used in all regions. Several natural colors of cotton occur, from white through reddish-brown and gray tones. These are used in designs much like the many natural shades of wool. Llama wool is coarse and usually yellow-brown. Alpaca is finer and softer than llama, in a wide range of shades from white through browns to black. Highly prized is the long, soft, wild vicuña wool — a natural golden yellow.

Equipment and weaves

Using crude equipment — backstrap looms, and possibly frames — these master weavers had a broad range of techniques, which they employed with competence and imagination. They achieved double cloths, tubular ribbons, brocades, pile knots, compound weaves, interlocked and slit tapestries, a distinctive warp-lock construction, repp, rigid warps, ginghams, netting, tassels, tufts, braids, embroideries, needle-knitting, painted fabrics, and even more.

FIGURE 2-56. Detail of Figure 2-54.

FIGURE 2-55. Peruvian interlocked tapestry belt. Same color, technique, and style as the border design in Figure 2-54. Tones of brown, with black limning. (Courtesy of Mrs. Charles Chapman.)

We are fortunate that so much has been preserved for us to see and study. Each year, more weavers are discovering these amazing fabrics through publications and in exhibitions. The sources for inspiration are almost inexhaustible. A careful study of the little figures in Peruvian textiles is rewarding. There is a sense of action — sometimes gaiety and playfulness; sometimes almost panic. A dynamic quality is there, similar to the aliveness found in Etruscan sculpture. Arms are gesturing, feet are running, mouths and eyes are expressive, and each creature has a definite personality. If you can get beyond a feeling of awe at the masterful craftsmanship in Peruvian textiles, you will enjoy looking at all of the elements of a design.

FIGURE 2-57. Fragment of interlocked tapestry, alpaca fabric with borders. Very colorful, with birds and stripes in black, yellow, blue-green, medium gold-brown, off-white, light and dark purple-red. Chimu. (Courtesy of the Seattle Art Museum, Eugene Fuller Memorial Collection.)

Examples of Peruvian weaving

The splendid alpaca rug shown in Figure 2-60 is unbelievably soft and silky, yet heavy and sturdy enough for a floor covering. Natural colors are from creamy white through several shades of light, warm beige and brown, to rich tones of chocolate brown to nearly black. The fine warp, almost completely covered, is gold and green.

Only when you hold the rug in your hands and look closely, are you aware that there is color in the warp.

Technique

Two strips, each 35 inches wide, are sewn together. The rug is 70 by 92 inches. Interlocked tapestry technique joins the

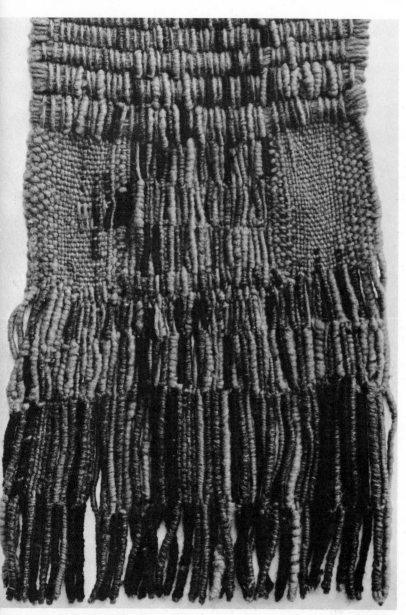

FIGURE 2-58. Wrapped weave, long wrapped warp fringe. Derived from Peruvian techniques. Wool. (Courtesy of Sheila Hicks, and *Handweaver & Craftsman*, New York.)

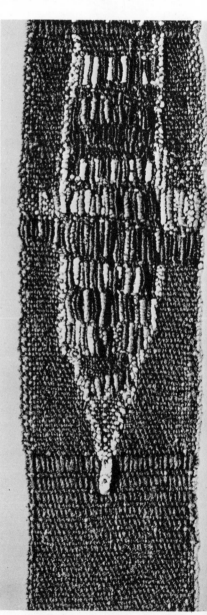

FIGURE 2-59. Plain weave and wrapped warp. Derived from Peruvian techniques. (Courtesy of Sheila Hicks, and *Handweaver & Craftsman*, New York.)

border colors to the white background. Medallions of interlocked tapestry are spaced over all of the rug.

Design

Here is a fine example of total design. The two strips of weaving were carefully planned to make the whole rug design complete. Each half has the border across the ends and down the outside edge. The rows of large patterns (5 by 6½ inches) alternate with seven or six medallions. Where there are seven in the row, the middle one is woven half on one strip, half on the other, so that a whole pattern is formed when the two strips are put together. The design also requires measuring while the work is in progress to match up the strips. The four design units, woven half and half, are almost perfectly matched. Borders are also lined up exactly for a continuous band on all four sides. The thin strips of dark brown are laid in orderly fashion throughout, and they, too, line up quite evenly.

FIGURES 2-60, 61, 62. Alpaca rug from Huancayo, Peru. Typical of weaving in Central Peru. Interlocked tapestry technique. Natural colors of alpaca wool, from white to a very dark brown. (Courtesy of Grace G. Denny, Professor Emeritus, University of Washington, Seattle.)

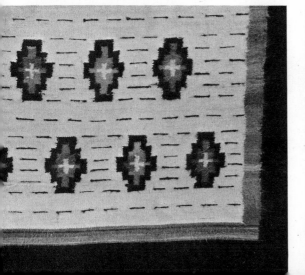
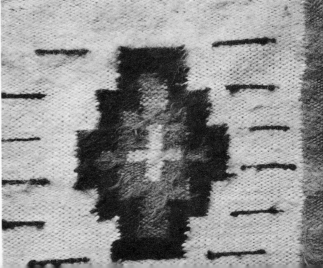

FIGURE 2-63. Detail of two combs in Figure 2-64.

Rigid warps

An air of mystery seems to surround the exact use of and precise method of weaving combs (2-63, 2-64). Their size and the spacing of the reeds indicate a possible use by weavers as beaters for fine fabric weaving. A rigid warp of smooth sticks or reeds is neatly even, and bound together with beautifully woven patterned bands of fine yarn. Each comb has a distinctive, tightly woven weft design. The sticks could have been split from a type of long, hollow cane. Colors in the woven bands are gold and black, a faded red and off-white, red and tan, brown and rust. One has small sticks wound with two colors, loosely attached to the front and back of the comb, above

FIGURE 2-64. Peruvian combs, rigid warp. An unusually large collection, all uniform in size. Notice the similarity of the checker-board one to the large square (Figure 2-65). Found near Lima, Peru. (Courtesy of Mrs. Charles Chapman.)

FIGURE 2-65. Fine-spun alpaca in several colors makes a checkered weft over a warp of reeds. (Courtesy of the Seattle Art Museum, gift of Nasli Heeramaneck.)

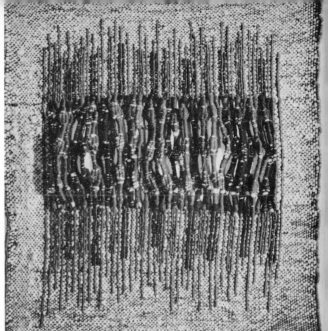

FIGURE 2-67. Plain weave and wrapped warp, wool. Derived from Peruvian techniques. 30 by 34 inches. (Courtesy of Sheila Hicks, and *Handweaver & Craftsman*, New York.)

and below the patterned weaving. The combs, found near Lima, Peru, are in excellent condition, although two show some signs of wear in the weft.

In Figure 2-65 a square of reed warp is covered with closely packed woven squares in several colors. Its exact use is unknown, but reed needle cases have been found with a similar rigid warp fabric as an outer covering. Flexible in only one direction, it could be used like our present-day bamboo screens and blinds.

A delicate, narrow band of interlocked tapestry is shown in Figure 2-66. Small black squares are placed to form a repeated pattern. Background colors shade from a light golden yellow through gold and brown and orange. It is only one-half an inch in width.

FIGURE 2-68. Early Chimu or Middle Nazca. The warp of this alpaca tapestry fabric is sewing-thread fine. Double bird pattern is repeated in each band, but with changing color combinations. Colors are off-white, dull gold, deep purple-red, black and a dark red-brown. (Courtesy of the Seattle Art Museum, Eugene Fuller Memorial Collection.)

FIGURE 2-66. Narrow band, interlocked tapestry technique. Peru. (Courtesy of Mrs. Charles Chapman.)

Indians of the Pacific Northwest

Two groups of Northwest Indians wove wool blankets of completely different types, each kind an interesting technique. The Chilkat Indians made blankets that were closely woven in a twining technique, of wool spun with a core of softened and shredded cedar bark. Wool was dyed black, soft yellow, and green-blue, and then used with a natural white wool. The Salish Indians made loosely woven blankets in a twill-like weave, of very coarse mountain goat wool, usually plain white. Sometimes a stripe or border of brown is put in.

Chilkat and Salish looms

Chilkat and Salish looms were similar — both vertical, with top and bottom beams inserted in slots, with space where wedges could be driven in to help control the tension of the warp. Salish loom uprights were driven into the ground. Chilkat loom uprights sat in blocks of wood. Their methods of fastening the warp to the loom, however, differed as much as their ways of weaving.

Chilkat blankets

More ornamental than utilitarian, Chilkat blankets are for ceremonial occasions. They are highly prized by collectors, who use them for wall hangings. Traditionally, women did the weaving; but since some of the designs are of a semireligious significance, supposedly unfamiliar to the women, men drew the designs in detail and made pattern boards for the women to follow. Because the designs were usually symmetrical, the pattern boards included the design for only one side (just past the middle).

FIGURE 2-69. Chilkat blanket. Very old, very well done. The colors are somewhat faded, but the light yellow and blue can still be seen. (Courtesy of Gene Zema. Photograph by Don Normark.) Shown in color on page 38.

Warps were cut different lengths, suspended from a warp beam at the top of the loom, and arranged in order to form the gradual curve at the bottom. A very long warp fringe, following the curve, hung straight without any extra knotting.

The weaving is a combination of two strand twining and tapestry weave. Units of design were woven separately, then joined. See Figure 2-71. The long, loose warp strands were divided and bundled into bags to keep them clean during the long process of weaving. The weight of the wool bundles probably helped keep some tension on the warp, and aided in the weaving. Unfortunately, the dust sheet covers the warp beam in our photograph of the Chilkat blanket in the beginning stages of weaving. You can see very clearly how the units of design are woven independently, and how the wool is gathered into neat little bags.

FIGURE 2-70. Chilkat blanket woven by, owned, and worn by members of the Killer Whale Clan of the Dukla-Wady tribe, Alaska. (Photograph by William L. Paul, Jr.)

FIGURE 2-71. Mary Williams, a member of the Raven Clan, sits beside her loom where she has begun to weave a Chilkat blanket. Klukwan, on the Chilkat River. (Photograph by William L. Paul, Jr.)

FIGURE 2-72. Salish loom, with a small sampling of warp and weaving. Note the scalloped carving on the upright members of the loom. The top and bottom beams are rollers, set in slots with room for wedges to be driven in when necessary to adjust the warp tension. Some Salish looms had several slots to adjust the beams for different size blankets. (Courtesy of the Thomas Burke Memorial Washington State Museum.)

FIGURE 2-73. Salish blanket, with materials and tools used by the weaver. Stick spindle, with whorl to keep the yarn from sliding off. Long wooden sword-like tool was used to pound fine white clay into the fibers. This much-prized white clay helped to degrease the wool, as well as whiten it. Materials are a cluster of goat hair, fireweed fluff sometimes mixed with the wool in spinning, and a ball of the fine white clay. (Courtesy of the Thomas Burke Memorial Washington State Museum.)

Salish blankets

Salish men carved and built the looms; the women did the weaving. The warp was put on in a special way, and woven so that the finished blanket had four selvages, and there were no cut edges to tie, hem, or sew. Sometimes a looped or twisted fringe was added just for decoration. The blankets are rectangular, about 5 feet long for a mantle, and as much as 10 feet or more when used for bedding.

The warp on a Salish loom is put over roller-beams, a loom-string is tied across, and the warp goes over this, then around, so that the finished blanket has a selvage on all four sides. The sketch in Figure 2-75 will give you an idea of how this is done. The weaving begins just below the loom-string, continues on down, and when the warp is covered to the bottom beam, the warp at the back is rolled around and the weaving is completed. After the weaving has been removed from the loom, the loom-string is taken out, and the blanket opens flat.

FIGURE 2-74. A Squamish Indian woman, weaving a blanket similar to the Salish blanket you find shown in Figure 2-73. On the top beam, you can just see the line where the loom string goes across (Figure 2-78). (Courtesy of the National Museum of Canada.)

FIGURE 2-75. Salish blankets are warped with a loom string arrangement. When the blanket is woven on all of the warp, the loom string is pulled out and the blanket opened out flat. All edges are selvages.

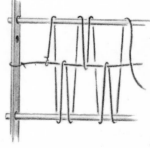

Navaho

Since the 1700's, the Navahos, American Indians of the Southwest, have been identified with weaving. Their handspun wool rugs and blankets are notable for their characteristic geometric designs and color groups.

The loom

An easily assembled — or dismantled — vertical loom was developed by these semi-nomadic people. They move from place to place with their flocks of sheep, and usually set up their looms out-of-doors. The weaver sits on the ground, often on a soft mound of sheepskin.

The yarn and the weaving

Yarn is spun on a shaft and whorl spindle. Natural black and white wools from their sheep are carded together, combining to produce all shades of gray. Some wool is dyed with vegetable dye; some colors are from commercial chemical dyes.

In the plain tapestry weave, at least four types of color joining are used. The lines and angles of the design dictate whether the color changes are made in a straight slit, diagonal slit, straight dovetail, or diagonal dovetail (see Chapter 8). Weft is beaten in very firmly, with a batten stick and/or a wooden comb. The beater combs are perfectly designed for their purpose. Teeth are cut into a thick section of wood; the long, tapered handle slants up at a slight angle, ending in a slightly rounded point. The thickness of the wood just above the teeth gives it weight, and helps to fit it to the hand for the best beating position. The pointed handle end is useful to beat in very small places. When the comb is set aside, the angle of the handle is such that it is readily picked up in the beating position. As if all of this efficiency is not enough, it is beautiful, too! Mine is of a satin smooth two-toned wood. This is an example of the truism that form following function equals beauty.

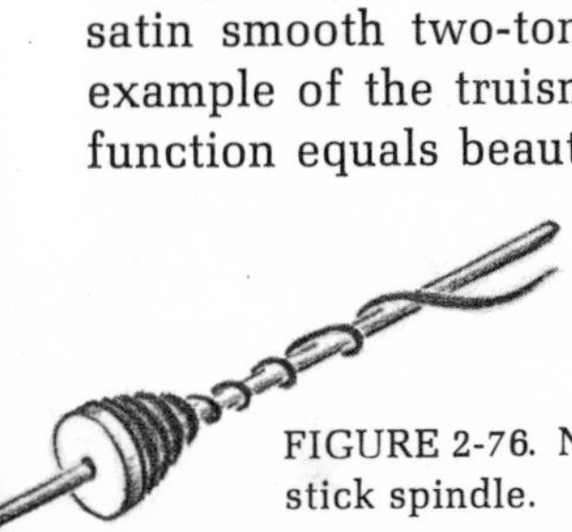

FIGURE 2-78. Navaho woman weaving a rug on her loom set up outside of her desert home. At the top left of the rug, note how the weaving has been continued up on a slant, several inches above the row being woven. In the foreground are cards for carding the wool, and a long spindle for spinning the wool into yarn. (Courtesy of Charles E. Little.)

FIGURE 2-79. Small Navaho loom, about saddle blanket size. (Courtesy of Charles E. Little.)

For further study of the Navaho

Much has been written about the development and history of Navaho weaving — colors, significance of designs, trading — as well as weaving and looms. We refer you to some of these in the Bibliography, and hope you will delve further into the study of these truly American weavings.

FIGURE 2-76. Navaho stick spindle.

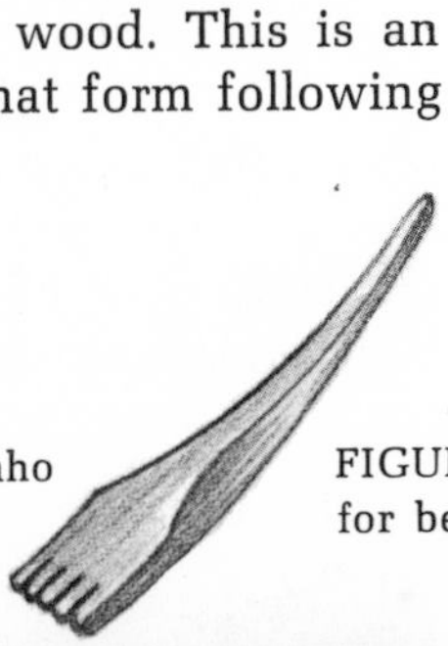

FIGURE 2-77. Navaho beater-comb for beating in the weft.

FIGURE 2-80. Bhotiya woman weaving a knotted rug on her loom set up out of doors. Handspun wool in natural shades of beige, brown, and black are combined with a red-brown obtained from walnut juice dye, along with some chemical dyes in brighter colors. The location is Munsiari, Almora District, Uttar Pradesh, India, on the border of India and Tibet. (Photograph by Elizabeth Bayley Willis.)

FIGURE 2-81. Bhotiya wool loom, and Bhotiya blanket. The weaver sits on a bear skin, rug, or woven mat, with feet in the pit, to weave on this pit loom. Strips of handspun wool are woven, then joined together, to make blankets with stripes of natural colored wools. (Photograph by Elizabeth Bayley Willis.)

FIGURE 2-82. The Ghana Kente cloth loom (Courtesy of Mrs. Ruth F. Williams. Photograph by *The Seattle Times*.)

Ghana loom

Men are the weavers in Ghana. They use this quite complicated looking loom to weave the narrow, colorful strips of cotton and silk that are sewn together to make robes, much like Roman togas. These robes are official dress in Ghana. Kente cloth (see Chapter 7) is woven with yarn as fine as sewing thread. Bands of geometric pattern alternate with plain weave. Boys learn to weave while quite young, using small looms. A full-size loom may be about 6 by 10 feet (2-82).

The weaver sits on the ground, with his feet in a pit. Metal disks suspended from each set of string heddles are inserted between the toes, to control the selection and movement of the heddles. Tension is maintained by piling stones on a flat sheet of metal, to which the warp is tied.

Coptic

A tapestry does not have to be wall-size to be a work of art. Neither does it have to be a wall decoration. Regard the exquisite Egyptian Coptic roundels and bands in extremely fine linen and wool yarns. With an admirable restraint, these beautifully woven little tapestries were applied to garments and vestments, which were made of plain weave cloth. These are not portraits, in the sense of trying to copy a painting in thread. They are a completely honest expression of the technique. The typical big eyes represent the technical limitations of weaving a very small circle on a few rigidly straight threads, and yet making the design expressive.

Just for fun, observe the eyes and how tapestry weavers solved the problem of weaving them in as many different kinds of tapestries as possible. There is a similarity in some Peruvian eyes and Coptic eyes. A vast difference will be noted between the so-called primitive weavings, and the faithfully realistic tapestries which are adapted from paintings.

FIGURE 2-84. Coptic roundel, 9 inches, fourth–fifth century. Linen warp. Weft is mostly black and white linen. Designs in circles are dull red-orange, gold, and green. (Courtesy of the Seattle Art Museum, Eugene Fuller Memorial Collection.)

FIGURE 2-83. Single, unsewn strips of Kente cloth show a variety of designs and colors. The two lighter ones have brilliant blue warp and unpatterned areas; the other, maroon warp and plain stripes. Both are patterned in white, gold, maroon, and blue. (Courtesy of Mrs. Ruth F. Williams. Photograph by *The Seattle Times*.)

FIGURE 2-85. Wool tapestry fragment, Egypt, third–fifth century. (Courtesy of the Seattle Art Museum, gift of the Seattle Weavers' Guild.)

FIGURE 2-86. Fifth century tapestry fragment. Linen warp and weft as fine as sewing thread. Only 8½ inches high, woven in great detail; light red, black, off-white, and blue-green. (Courtesy of the Seattle Art Museum, Eugene Fuller Memorial Collection.)

FIGURE 2-87. Coptic, tapestry technique, 15 inches long. Rich purple wool and off-white linen, on a white linen warp. (Courtesy of the Seattle Art Museum, gift of Nasli Heermaneck.)

FIGURE 2-88. This tapestry loom, built for Lois Clarke by Luther Hooper in London some years ago, has a weaving limit of 10 inches wide and 30 inches in length. Using extremely fine wools and silks, and working from carefully scaled and detailed cartoons, Miss Clarke has specialized in weaving miniature tapestries. (Courtesy of Miss Lois Clarke. Photograph by Tassone Studio.)

FIGURE 2-89. The zodiac signs and symbols. The background colors were determined when research revealed that six symbols belonged to day and six to night. Colors were also prescribed for the symbols. Woven by Lois Clarke. Cartoon by Gladys G. Young. (Courtesy of Miss Lois Clarke. Photograph by Whitestone Photo.)

FIGURE 2-90. Swedish Knot Tapestry. Simple, but very effective. Two colors — black tree, spring green background. Wool on a cotton warp. (Courtesy of Gladys McIlveen.)

FIGURE C-12. A PACIFIC OCEAN BEACH.
(Photograph by Ron Wilson.)

FIGURE C-18. A flowering
plum tree, floodlighted.
(Photograph by Gary Wilson.)

FIGURE C-13. PHILIPPINE RICE TERRACES.
(Photograph by Randy Davidson.)

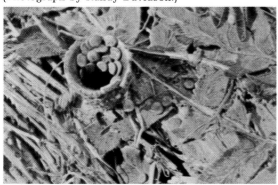

FIGURES C-14, 15, 16, 17. MUSHROOMS AND FUNGUS. (Photographs by Frances Sharpe.)

3 Tapestry

Tapestry is a technique or a method of weaving a weft-faced, ribbed, patterned fabric. The design is identical on both sides; the warp is completely covered. Wefts do not go from edge to edge, but colors are joined at the pattern areas. A true tapestry has to be woven by hand. Tapestry weaving does seem a little mysterious, until you learn that the true tapestry weave is a plain weave. The special names for different kinds of tapestries evolve from a country, an area, or the people weaving them. Sometimes the name comes from the special method used in the weaving.

Weavers are apt to be humbled by the very word tapestry, as they immediately think of the huge, infinitely detailed and shaded European tapestries. The techniques are basically simple, and small looms and frames are perfectly adequate for beginners weaving small pieces and samplers to master the methods. (See Projects, Chapter 8.) A tapestry is generally understood to be a pictorial weaving. The word is mistakenly used to describe almost any kind of a wall hanging or woven design, regardless of whether a tapestry technique or a combination of methods has been used. The most famous of misnomers is the wondrous Bayeux Tapestry, which is really an embroidery on woven cloth.

KNOT–TYPE TAPESTRIES

Various warp-encircling techniques are used in knot-type tapestries. They fit the definition of tapestry, except that the weft goes around each warp thread instead of passing over it. Four of these techniques, Swedish knot, Egyptian, Soumak, and Greek Soumak are discussed in this chapter, along with directions on how to do them. Swedish knot is my personal favorite, but I feel that all of them are important. Learn them all, as well as the true tapestry technique and color changes, and you will have a rich source to draw from when you weave.

FIGURES 3-1,2. Two plain weave tapestries, but what a difference in their appearance! 3-1, Coptic sixth–seventh century. Bishops' vestments. Extremely fine yarn, minutely detailed. The stoles are just 28 inches long, center panel, 13 inches wide, and the two roundels only 8 inches. (Courtesy of the Seattle Art Museum, Eugene Fuller Memorial Collection.) 3-2, Norwegian geometric tapestry. All of the ends are woven in so that the reverse side is exactly like the right side. Fine wool, very closely packed. (Courtesy of Mrs. V. L. Georgeson, weaver.)

FIGURE 3-3. Detail of Swedish knot tapestry. Also see Figure C-2, page 19. Note that this was woven with the design on its side. The ridges are therefore horizontal; in Figure 3-4, below, the ridges are vertical. Woven by the author.

FIGURE 3- 4. To point the way to her sons' rooms, Mary Hanson used a bit of whimsy. Woven in the Swedish knot technique, of very fine wool. Off-white background, banker's gray sleeve and snowy cuff outlined in black, set off the deep suntan color of the hand. Mary Hanson is a long-time weaver, but this was her first tapestry. (Courtesy of Mary Hanson. Photograph by Hans L. Jorgensen.)

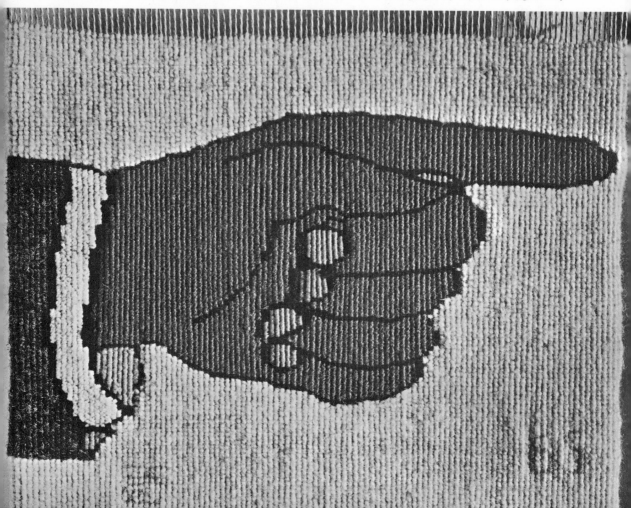

FIGURE 3-5. CIRCUS TENTS. Charming example of tapestries in our time. Plain weave, tapestry technique, knots and loops. Warp of many sizes and colors — mostly red, orange, and yellow; weft of several threads used as one so that the multicolored warp is not entirely covered. Suspension by the tent tops makes the finish and hanging an important part of the planned design. (Courtesy of the American Craftsmen's Council, Sally Adams, weaver. Photograph by Jerome Drown.)

HOW TAPESTRY TECHNIQUES GOT THEIR NAMES

An absorbing study is that of discovering the similarities and differences in the many named kinds of tapestry. You will find that while nearly identical methods are used in many countries, or by craftsmen in sections of a country, each technique will have its own name. The methods will vary in detail, but the basic technique will be the same. Differences may lie in the kind of bobbin, shuttle, needle- or finger-controlled method of putting in the weft; or a unique spin, twist, ply, weight, or kind of yarn or fiber. The warp may be fine, coarse, closely set, wide-spaced; and of cotton, linen, wool, silk, or another fiber. Design,

weaving pattern, colors, and combinations of colors will be original and unlike any others.

TRACING NAME ORIGINS

A Navaho rug is woven with coarsely handspun wool on a distinctively assembled vertical loom. An interlocked tapestry technique and symbolic Indian designs and colors are employed. Readily identified, these rugs are known as Navaho weaving. In Peru, Nazcas, the people of a culture dating from 2000 B. C., wove with finely handspun wool on backstrap looms. The designs are distinctly recognizable as theirs alone. The appearance of this Peruvian tapestry weaving (as it is now known) is completely different from the Navaho weaving, although both utilize the same basic technique. It is fun to match techniques, and then discover the different avenues of approach to the looms, weaving, and design.

TAPESTRIES IN OUR TIME

This weaver believes that in our day of photographic records of events and costumes, it is not as important to report the scene faithfully in the medium of tapestry weaving, as it was in early days. Then, there was some reason for paintings copied in yarn, or scenes and legends chronicled in fabric, to be used for wall decorations and warmth in drafty rooms. The tapestries were handed down from generation to generation. Now we no longer need to weave our own fabrics for clothing and household; we are free to weave what we choose in our tapestries and wall hangings. We can express in yarns a mood or impression, a favorite color and texture idea. Endless years, quantities of expensive material, and dozens of people need no longer be involved. This can be a very personal experience. There is so much to explore in so many directions. Look backward as well as forward. Design, weave, savor, enjoy yourself! Learn the techniques, then you will know how to do what you prefer, within the limits of warp and weft.

DESIGN

The weaver chooses whether a tapestry design is woven on its side or vertically. Plain weave, Swedish knot, and Egyptian knot are characterized by definite ridges running in the direction of the warp. Consider that when the tapestry is woven and hung, its structural strength will be greater if the warp is horizontal and the weft is vertical. Because the warp is widely spaced and the weft is so tightly woven, the strength is in the weft.

Also, choose to weave in the direction with fewer color joinings. If there are many long lines of unbroken color, place the design on the warp so that these will be

woven across the warp, instead of being joined vertically. See the five small tapestries that follow on page 62.

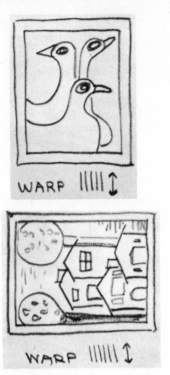

FIGURE 3-6. Warp direction in relation to design, tapestry weaving.

FIGURE 3-7. TEMPTATION. Detail of miniature tapestry woven by Lois Clarke. Cartoon by Elizabeth MacKinstry. (Courtesy of Miss Lois Clarke. Photograph by Helga Photo Studio, Inc.)

FIGURE 3-8. Oriental Soumak. Raw silk, creamy white; wool, dark brown; a few accents of red-orange, olive-green and gold. Designs adapted from Mexican flat stamp patterns. Woven by the author.

FIGURE 3-9. Wall hanging of very heavy linen, plain weave, loops, slit tapestry technique. Woven by the author. (Photograph by Art Hupy.)

FIGURE 3-10.Plain weave tapestry.

FIGURE 3-11.Plain weave tapestry.

APPLICATION OF TAPESTRY TECHNIQUES

To show you how different tapestry techniques affect the looks of one design, we gave ourselves this problem:

> Weave five tapestries on small frames — $5^{1}/_{2}$ by $7^{1}/_{2}$ inches. Use the same design for all. For each tapestry, limit yourself to five colors. We chose dark brown, white, light yellow, deep gold, and gray-green.

Use these different techniques and methods, to illustrate what happens:

> Make some in plain weave tapestry, and others in Swedish-knot tapestry.

Try interlocking of colors three ways:

> 1. Use the dovetail method of color interlock, as an element of the design.
> 2. Use limning, which is outlining, in a contrasting color.
> 3. Use the slit technique, with the slit being part of the design.

On some, include interlocked borders.

> Try one with open warp background, combined with solid areas. Weave one with the warp at right angles to your design (the design will be sideways). Include dots, spots, lines, and blended shades in the background. Use only one or two of these ideas in any one piece.

EXAMPLES OF THE DIFFERENT TAPESTRIES

Here they are, and this was such fun to do that we highly recommend it to you as a sampling idea. By the time the fifth one was under way, we were just a little tired of those big-eyed water birds, but learned many lessons in this effort.

In this plain weave tapestry (3-10), dovetail interlocking is used on the necks to suggest feathers, and to make an interesting vertical line. There is interlock joining where the lines are straight, woven over pairs of warp.

Here, the plain weave tapestry (3-11) has slit borders on each side. Outlining is in white, and the slits are interlocked about every half inch. The weaving is done over pairs of warp.

This plain weave tapestry (3-12) is woven with the design on its side. Almost no interlocking is required. The background is over single warp threads; the birds over two warp threads. Ridged tapestry is woven with horizontal and larger stitches to give birds a feathered look.

FIGURE 3-12.Plain weave tapestry.

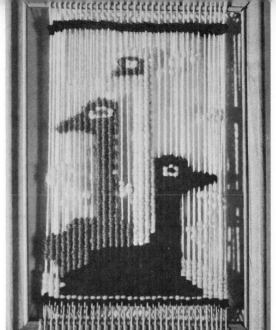

FIGURE 3-13.Swedish knot tapestry.

The Swedish knot tapestry (3-13) is woven over pairs of warp threads. The background is left as open warp, except for a few casual spots. The rows woven at top and bottom hold the warp in place.

Again, the Swedish knot tapestry (3-14) is woven over pairs of warp threads. It is interlocked where necessary, to avoid slits, especially in long verticals of the necks. Single knots make the dots. Two shades in the upper background are curved and blended. (Refer to the how-to-do-it information later in the chapter.)

CONCLUSIONS

Little tapestries like this are invaluable as samplers. You can do just about anything in a tapestry technique, within the structural limits of warp and weft. Thoroughly learn all of the techniques, then you can do what you like with them. If you prefer to weave in the classic, traditional manner of a particular type of tapestry, you will follow the prescribed rules for that. You select the correct warp and weft yarns, the setting per inch, the weaving and interlock methods, the type of design and colors. It is the weaver's choice!

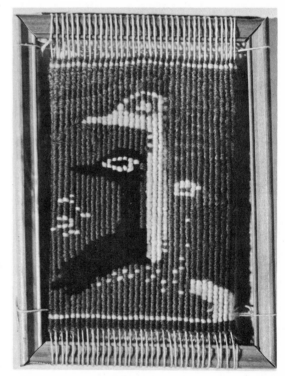

FIGURE 3-14. Swedish knot tapestry.

DESIGNING

Your first few tapestries should be simple, designed to show you the weaving problems involved. When the methods and limitations are learned, you can go on to more intricate and detailed weaving. Our technique examples were woven and chosen to show in an uncomplicated way, what is happening; where and how to begin. Our historical and present day examples will show you what can be done if these same basic methods are used.

Cartoon

A tapestry design, drawn on paper in detail, with notes on color, actually colored or shaded with pencil, is called a cartoon. Correctly, it should be fastened behind the warp so that the weaver can follow the design. On a small loom, since the cartoon may just get in the way, you may prefer to ink your design on the warp.

Inking a design on the warp

Place your cartoon under the warp, fastening with paper clips or tape. Be sure to use waterproof ink, so that there will be no possibility of ink smears if you dampen your tapestry for blocking. Hold the pen point against the warp, and twist the thread around and back between thumb and first finger so that the line of ink goes around the warp thread. Since the threads twist slightly as you weave, you want to be sure that the design outline is clear. If your design is simple, and as you become more experienced in this kind of weaving, you will find that just a few key lines of the design are all that you need on the warp. Be sure that the design lines show on the side of the warp you weave from — right or wrong. Also, check to see that the design is facing the right way from the finished side. This checking is especially important when numbers or letters are in your design.

Some weavers do not use a cartoon, or even a sketch, but weave beautiful, free-wheeling hangings. This takes experience and vision. If you plan a tapestry with many lines and color changes, you should

FIGURE 3-15. Design cartoon for tapestry, shaded and outlined.

have a drawing beside you for easy reference. We do recommend that you prepare a cartoon or a simple sketch for a guide.

"Trees," used for the Frontispiece, literally just grew from an experiment with a technique. Curious to see what Swedish knot looked like on a wide-spaced, very coarse warp, with a heavy handspun wool weft, I tried it. The colors at hand were shades of green and gold. When about an inch or so of Swedish knot was woven, the exaggerated ribbing suggested tree trunks. From there on, the trees took over. The idea of sky-blue shades between the trunks to give depth seemed like a good one, but the open spaces proved to be much more effective. Because of the openings, the work needed to have tension sustained. A frame of dowels and strips was contrived, with the warp looped over small brads. The bottom of the frame was left movable until the proper tension was obtained. A small brad was put in on each side to hold the bottom strip firm. This same finished effect could be accomplished by weaving in a frame, with nails to hold warp on the back of the frame.

WARP

As tapestry is a weft-faced weave, warp should be widely spaced. Six, eight, up to thirteen threads per inch will work well, always depending upon the weight of the warp thread, the fineness of detail desired, the method of weaving used and the weight of the weft yarn. Sometimes two warp threads are woven as one, in pairs. Six or eight threads to the inch are a good number for a beginning tapestry weaver. You will be able to see just where the weft goes in relation to the warp. For fine detail and small stitches, have the warp closely spaced. For a bold design with large areas of one color, use coarser warp, fewer per inch. Traditionally, tapestry warp is linen or wool. For small tapestries, cotton is satisfactory. The warp must be strong. It must be smooth enough for the weft to slip over and cover readily. Do not use a fuzzy or loosely spun warp, for the weft will not cover well, and little hairs of warp will show, especially with a light warp and dark weft. Carpet warp, smooth linen, wool worsted, seine twine are all good tapestry warps. In a wall hanging where much of the warp might be left unwoven, threads can be chosen for texture and color and unusual spins, as they will be part of the total design. See "Bird Heads," Figure 3-16, C-6.

Warp can be any color in a tapestry, since it will be covered. If a light color is used, you can see at once where the weft has not covered. If a dark color is used, you might not have to pack in quite so much weft.

A tapestry weaver commissioned to do several large works on a very limited budget, took advantage of this. The warp was colored to match or blend in with large areas. The weft could just barely cover, but the overall effect was of solid color. The work went faster, the design and color were true, and the budget was met.

WEFT

Wool is by far the most satisfactory material for weft, because it packs in so easily, and the effect is of rich color and texture. Wool is traditionally used for weft in tapestries. Put the weft in so that it is slack

enough to push down and cover all of the warp. See "bubbling" in Chapter 1.

When you depart from the true way of weaving tapestry, you are free to use any warp or weft for the look you want. Work within the boundaries of the technique, and do not try to weave a smooth tapestry from a nubby yarn.

FIGURE 3-16. BIRD HEADS. Open weave, tapestry technique. Deep and bright blues and greens of sky, water, and feathers. Woven by the author.

- Unless otherwise noted, all tapestries discussed are woven from the bottom up.
- Sometimes it may be that you will need only your fingers to work in a short length of weft. Do feel free to get the job done in a comfortable and efficient way for you. Learn the proper way to do it, and how it should look; then relax and produce it the best way you can.
- Do not weave too far up on a unit of color without bringing the adjoining areas of color along too. Check the slant of design lines to be sure you will not have an awkward space to fill below an overhang. Constantly check the points where color changes occur to keep from weaving beyond a change point.
- When directions say to weave with the right side or the wrong side up, you will find that way is the best for that technique. At first it will seem impossible to weave from the wrong side, but you will soon realize it is easier.
- When the weaving is finished, weave in a few extra rows at the top for a protective heading so that your woven work is in no danger of ravelling.
- Before removing the finished weaving from the loom you can further protect it in one of several ways: run a line of colorless glue (Elmer's, No-Sew) along, and make sure that each warp thread is covered. Let it dry thoroughly, then cut the warp and your weaving edge will be safely held in place. Or sew a running stitch or overcast stitch along the last row of weaving. Cut just a few warp threads at a time, tie in a knot securely against the last row of weaving. Continue to cut and tie across the width.
- To finish the edges, you can have a plain hem. For this, turn back the headings, top and bottom, and hem down. Or you can sew tape along the raw edge, with machine or by hand, trim warp ends, turn back, and hem down.
- Edges may be enhanced with decorative borders or rows of needle stitches. Plan these along with the woven part of the design. Knots, stitches, braids, fringe —

anything goes in a wall hanging, just as long as it is in keeping with the total design. Traditionally, tapestry is simply turned back and hemmed or lined, with no visible means of hanging.

Hanging

The selection of a hanger will depend upon the whole look of the woven hanging. Wooden poles, metal rods, interesting knobby sticks, bamboo, strips of wood — anything can be used — but it should be an extension of the work it is to show. For example, an unpeeled, knotty stick is totally out of character at the top of a finely woven, pastel-colored hanging. It is just as disturbing to see a delicate, pale stem of bamboo attempting to hold up a bold and beautiful wall hanging of large seed pods and stems. A rod or sturdy strip of wood can be run through hems, to provide an invisible but strong hanger. An elaborately braided or knotted top and bottom could be the most important part of a hanging, with just a small woven section in the center.

Blocking

To square up and flatten your tapestry, you may use one of several methods to block it.

1. Thoroughly soak the tapestry in water; shape and pin it to the shape you want. Let it dry thoroughly. If you do this, be very sure that your yarns are colorfast and that ink used for a design on the warp is waterproof.

2. Pin the weaving to a padded surface, face down. Use an ironing board, floor, or a table top which has been protected so that steam and heat will not damage it. Place a dampened cloth over the weaving, and steam with a hot iron. Do not use pressure, for this will flatten and spoil the texture of the weaving. Do not use a scrubbing motion, or the weaving will become distorted. Remove the cloth, allow to dry thoroughly before lifting.

3. If no real blocking is necessary, lightly press on the back with a steam iron and a

dry cloth. Some wall hangings will need no pressing, and can be hung up right from the loom.

RELATED TAPESTRY KNOT TECHNIQUES

Four knot techniques are related: Swedish knot, Egyptian knot, Oriental Soumak, and Greek Soumak. Their similarities are that they each encircle the warp; they are all like needle stitches; (i. e., they are more easily woven with needle than shuttle, and frequent, minute color changes are possible); they are interlocked to avoid slits; and they all are used for rugs and tapestries.

Comparisons

HOW TO WEAVE	SWEDISH KNOT	ORIENTAL SOUMAK	GREEK SOUMAK	EGYPTIAN TAPESTRY KNOT
One complete stitch	1 knot over 1 warp	Over 4 warps, back 2	1 knot over 1 warp, *but* 3 knots on same warp	1 knot over 1 warp
Weave	Wrong side up	Right side up	Right side up	Right side up
Weaving direction in any one piece	Left and/or right	Left and/or right	Left or right	Left and/or right
Rows, areas	Either	Rows	Rows	Either
Ends of weft	Left hanging	Darned in or tied	Tied	Left hanging or tied
Number of warps per inch	6–12	6–12	6–12	6–12
Slits	No	No	No	No
Interlock	Yes	Yes	Yes	Yes
Weight of Fabric	Solid, firm	Variable; can be very heavy for rugs or looser for other purposes	Firm; slightly flexible. More or less open. Depends on how firmly pulled each knot is.	Firm
Surface Texture	Ribbed, in direction of warp	Slant like a twill, or a herringbone pattern, controlled by direction of stitch	Ribbed, in direction of warp on wrong side	Ribbed in direction of warp

SWEDISH KNOT TAPESTRY TECHNIQUE

Perhaps not quite as well known as the plain weave tapestry, this tapestry technique is called Swedish knot, or French-Swedish knot. Apparently it is not recognized as a technique from Sweden. The naming of it may be obscure, but the method fulfills many of the requirements of a tapestry technique definition: the warp is completely covered, areas of pattern are worked separately, there are no woven rows between knotted rows, and it is worked with the reverse side up. Where color changes occur in a vertical line, the yarn is interlooped to avoid a slit. Although the method is much like needlework in that each knot is worked separately with a bobbin or tapestry needle, it is weaving because it is worked over warp threads. It is a knot in the sense that the weft is wrapped completely around the warp. The right side appears to be a series of ridges following the direction of the warp. Since each warp encirclement is a complete knot, a color change can be made on every warp thread if required. Large areas can be covered with a continuous weft of one color. (For working directions, see Chapter 8.)

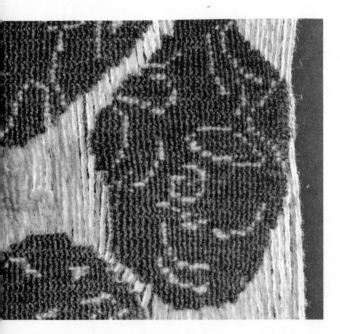

FIGURE 3-17. Detail of Figure 4-14. Swedish knot technique. (Courtesy of Gladys McIlveen, weaver.)

Advantages

Swedish knot tapestry can be done on the simplest frame, with no special tools needed. It requires no heddle or special bobbins or shuttles. It is a most portable kind of weaving, as the frames are lightweight and can be carried about easily. Therefore, this type of weaving is excellent for convalescents, vacationers, and fireside weavers.

Unlimited color changes are possible, and there is a pleasant rhythm in doing the knots. It is fascinating to see the design grow, dot by dot. Since very short lengths of yarn can be used — just long enough to make the knot, a desired accent of color or added line can be inserted quite easily with a needle, even though the design is completed. Also, a mistake can be taken out and corrected, even after the section has been covered. The yarn can be carefully picked out, cut off, and the correction knots put in with a needle.

Many articles besides tapestry wall hangings can be made with this method: chair seats, handbags, glasses cases, small purses, pillow tops — anything that can be woven to an exact size, that does not have to be cut and sewn, and that can have the shaggy reverse side hidden or lined.

Disadvantages

There are two disadvantages. The technique is comparatively slow; and more yarn is required than in plain weaving, because each warp thread is encircled, and so many ends are cut and left hanging.

GREEK SOUMAK

Greek Soumak knot technique makes a sturdy fabric with a rather coarse texture. This is a very good choice for small upholstery, pillows, big handbags, pictorial tapestry, or wall hangings. For upholstery, handbags, or pillows, it should be firmly and closely woven, but not so solidly packed that the very small openings between the triple knots are lost. When held to the light, you should see tiny pinpoint openings in the weave. Our example in Figure

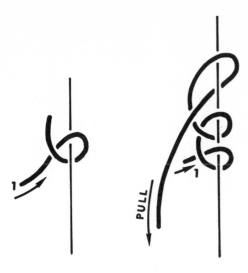

FIGURE 3-18. Greek Soumak knot. A, Method of making the knot. B, Three knots, one above the other on the same warp, make one complete knot.

FIGURE 3-19. Greek Soumak tapestry technique. Folded over to show reverse side. (Courtesy of Mrs. V. L. Georgeson, weaver.)

3-19 is extremely firm. Use where fabric does not have to be cut to shape or folded over in a hem. Greek Soumak can be used to make a fairly open fabric. The openings can be planned as a part of the design. Weave a combination of solid and open areas. Try using several strands of yarn for the coarse part; single strands tightly pulled for finer areas. Try six knots on one warp for larger holes. Play with the technique and see what effects you can achieve!

To learn the Greek Soumak knot technique, study the drawings in Figure 3-18. Start at 1, and follow the arrows. Put the weft around the warp in exactly the same way as for the Swedish knot, but work three knots around the same warp thread before going on to the next warp thread. Do not beat in. The pulling down to tighten the knot will be enough to put it in place. The density of the fabric can be controlled somewhat by slightly pushing the succeeding rows together. If rows are beaten in, your material will be stiff and board-like. Because the working surface is the right side, the reverse will look exactly like the Swedish knot tapestry, which is woven with the wrong side up. Figure 3-19 shows both sides.

ORIENTAL SOUMAK

Soumak, a type of Oriental rug, is believed to be one of the earliest forms of rug weaving. The technique is quite a simple one, like an embroidered stem stitch, except that it is worked over a warp. There is no rule stating how many warp threads are involved in a soumak stitch, but studies of antique carpets reveal that the usual plan is over four warp threads, and back two (3-20). It may be a solid one color weave or patterned like tapestry (3-21). Since a

FIGURE 3-20. Method of making Oriental Soumak.

row of plain weave between soumak rows will prevent slits, the patterns will require no interlocking. (If the plain weave rows are omitted, some interlocking may be necessary.)

Two very different surface effects are possible with this stitch. If each row is started at the same side of the warp, all of the stitches will slant in the same direction and look like a diagonal twill. If one row is made from right to left, then the next row returns from left to right, the second row will slant in the opposite direction to give a herringbone or knitted effect. Soumak is worked with the right side up, with a very small shuttle, or more conveniently, a tapestry needle. It can be woven without the rows of plain weave between, in a wall hanging, perhaps, but a rug needs the added strength and firmness of the woven rows.

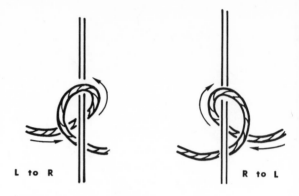

L to R   R to L

FIGURE 3-22. Method of making Egyptian tapestry knot.

EGYPTIAN TAPESTRY KNOT

This is a very good choice of technique for weaving pillows, cushions for small chair seats, or covers for footstools where needlepoint is usually used, and where the weaving will be used in the same size as woven. The weft completely encircles each warp thread. The surface is corded. Work with the right side up, weaving in either direction, or alternating from right to left, left to right. Interlock where color changes are made. The ends may be left hanging or tied.

To make the Egyptian tapestry knot (3-22): from left to right take weft yarn under the warp, up and over to the left; down under the warp to the right; pull down to tighten. The weft is wrapped around the warp. Then continue under the next warp to the right, to begin the next knot. Study the drawings and follow the path of the weft from right to left. Note that the weft is always on top of the warp at the top of the loop, and under the warp on both of the down-swings. See the comparison chart of tapestry knot techniques in this chapter.

FIGURE 3-21. Detail of Figure 3-8. Woven by the author.

SAMPLER — PLAIN WEAVE TAPESTRY

Before plunging in to make a large or finished piece of tapestry, we urge you to make samplers of each method. These can be small, separate pieces, later put together and mounted as a collage, or one large composition showing many methods. You can design this to be an attractive wall decoration in itself, as well as a valuable reference. Plan your colors and rows or areas of different techniques to blend into a pleasing whole. You will probably discover that one method pleases you most, or works best for you. Then, you can do your first real piece of tapestry in the technique you prefer.

A design can be very effective with just a few colors. Separate small samplers woven on small frames in correlated colors and sizes can be composed into one pictorial panel which can be hung as a wall decoration. On a practice warp, learn to do the interlocking, outlining, and knot techniques with confidence. When you know the limitations and demands of your technique, you can design a tapestry suited to the method. In all kinds of weaving, once you learn and are comfortable doing it, the work goes smoothly.

Color changes

Each method of color change creates its own distinct pattern or look. Choose the color change method to suit your total design — to emphasize some lines, to minimize others. (See Figures 3-10 to 3-14 for five small samplers.)

A plan for you to follow

Weave a dozen samples of tapestry technique. Weave at least an inch, preferably more of each of the following:

Six examples of ways to make color changes in plain weave tapestry.
One way to outline a design.
Example of hatching.
Three tapestry knot techniques.
Example of Soumak.

Learning all of these will give you a good basis of technique. You will have a selec-

FIGURE 3-23. SUGAR DOLLS. Plain weave tapestry. One of the tapestries woven by Egyptian children of Harrania. (Courtesy of *Handweaver & Craftsman*, New York.)

tion of methods to choose from when you weave a tapestry, or some other work. There are many more variants, and if you wish to pursue a further study, we refer you to the Bibliography.

Flat or plain weave tapestry

Flat or plain weave tapestry construction is simply weaving weft over and under warp threads, with the warp completely covered. The warp is set far enough apart so that the soft wool weft will push down and fill in, with no warp showing. Five to ten warp threads per inch is the usual number, depending upon the coarseness of the yarn used, and the scale of the design. The surface will be flat and smooth, but ridges show where the warp is. Traditionally, warp is linen, cotton, or wool. The weft is wool. An essential part of plain tapestry weaving is learning just how to beat in the rows of weaving so that the warp is completely covered. Wool, because of its softness and flexibility, is most satisfactory.

FIGURE 3·24. Animated tapestry of handspun wool. Woven by African pupils at Marjorie Pope Ellis School of Weaving, in Sabantu Village, Pietermarutzburg. (Courtesy of Ruby W. Burkheimer. Photograph by Fortescue.)

The trick is to have the weft relaxed just enough to lie flat, but not to bump up between the warp threads. The perfection of this technique comes with practice. Use the drawing of how to bubble the weft (6-16), and try it. A firm, pressing-down motion is more effective here than a sharp beating. Pushing down short segments across the warp is also helpful.

What you will need to weave your tapestry sampler

You should have a frame loom with inside opening of approximately 10 by 15 inches. The size will depend upon how you want to weave your samples. If you want to do a dozen on one warp, allow a minimum of 1 inch for each one, plus an inch for headings. Warp of 6 by 14 inches will provide enough space for a small sampling of each.

Your warp should be cotton carpet warp, or linen. The weft should be wool worsted, in at least two colors, one dark, one light. You will also need tapestry needles or a small stick shuttle, scissors, a ruler, and a pencil.

How to warp

Put a warp 6 inches wide, with ten warp threads to each inch. See Warping, in Chapter 6. The warp should run the long way of the frame.

What to weave

Weave ½-inch plain weave, over and under, one color, for the heading. Weave at least 1 inch of the following interlock techniques. Use two colors so that you can see just how the color changes are made.

INDIVIDUAL CHARACTERISTICS OF THE COLOR CHANGE TECHNIQUES

Straight slit (Kilim)

Where the slits occur, there will be a straight, clean line. Short vertical openings can be used as part of the design to give another dimension, or to create a pattern of slits (3-25). Slits should be carefully planned so that the structure of the fabric will not be weakened.

Diagonal slit

Clear cut, smooth-edged areas of color are formed when the weft is stepped up and over just one warp at a time. There is no joining or interlocking. Tiny holes will be made when more than one row is woven before stepping over, but often these are only visible when the fabric is held to the light. They can be made a part of the design, and deliberately exaggerated by weaving several rows before going over and up (3-26).

Straight interlock

With this method, there is a minimum of thickness at the joining line. To keep it smooth, always loop the wefts around each other in the same order. The joining line may be quite straight or slightly jagged, depending upon how closely beaten the weft is, and what size yarn you are using.

Diagonal interlock

This is most useful when the design unit must be stepped over after several rows are woven, and you do not want any hole at all.

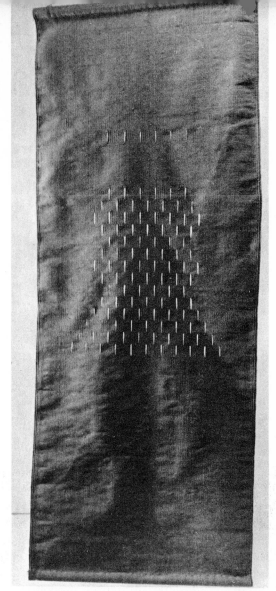

FIGURE 3-25. Wool textile. Tapestry technique with slits forming the design. (Courtesy of Sheila Hicks.)

Straight dovetail

Dovetail can be a very important and decorative part of your design. When you want a definite rick-rack or deep-toothed outline, weave and return several rows of weft. See how we used dovetail in this way to suggest a feathered outline on the water bird tapestry (3-10, C-4).

Diagonal dovetail

Diagonal dovetail can be used in the same way as the straight dovetail to make toothed outlines. Try it for making rooftops or stylized trees.

Straight slit

One weft enters from the left (3-26A), the other from the right. Weft yarn turns around adjacent warps and returns, leaving a slit. The two wefts do not interlock.

Diagonal slit

The two weft colors turn around adjacent warps and return (3-26B), but step over one warp thread at a time, on a slant. These are not noticeable slits, especially if only two rows are woven before stepping over.

Straight interlock

The two weft colors are carried toward (3-26C), then away from each other. They meet *between* two warp threads, loop around each other, and return. Colors are interlocked in each row of weaving as required by the design; areas are not built up independently. To keep the joining line smooth, always loop the wefts around each other in the same direction and order.

Diagonal interlock

Interlocking is made on a diagonal line (3-26D) by stepping over one warp thread to the right or left. When only a few rows of weaving are involved, the simpler method of the diagonal slit can be used just as well.

Straight dovetail

The dovetail method reverses each color around a common warp (3-26E), but the wefts do not loop around each other. Each weft is independent of and separate from the other wefts in the row. The colors alternate. As the method is like laying bricks, it sometimes is called brick-interlocking.

Diagonal dovetail

Dovetail on a diagonal reverses each weft color around a common warp (3-26F), but each succeeding row steps over one warp. The step-over can be made to right or left, or in zigzag fashion.

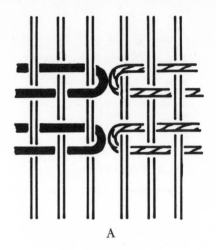

A

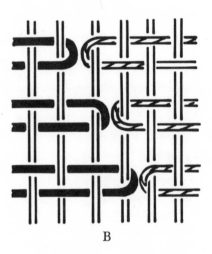

B

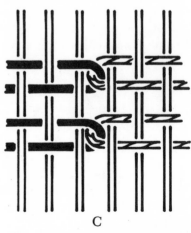

C

FIGURE 3-26. Methods of making color changes and joinings; plain weave tapestry techniques. A, Straight slit. B, Diagonal slit. C, Straight interlock. D, Diagonal interlock. E, Straight dovetail. F, Diagonal dovetail.

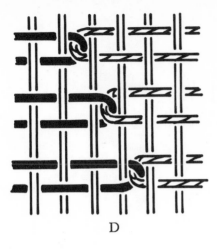

D

Hatching

Hatching is a blending of color lines. A row of weft is taken part way across, interlocked with a second color, in the same row, and returned. Rows of various lengths are woven in this fashion to give an uneven, sketchy look. Effective in a large background area where a single color would be uninteresting and flat, a hatching of several tones gives life to an otherwise plain section. Figures 3-27 and 3-28 show examples of two methods of hatching: either with thick and thin lines, or with triangular, flame-like points.

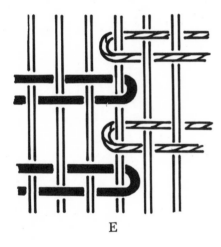

E

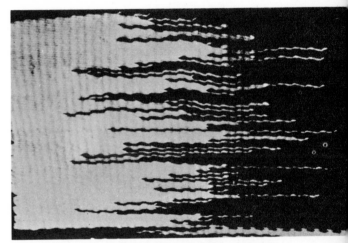

FIGURE 3-27. Hatching. Tapestry technique. (Courtesy of Clydene Phelps, weaver. Photograph by Clydene Phelps.)

FIGURE 3-28. Hatching. (Courtesy of Mrs. V. L. Georgeson, weaver.)

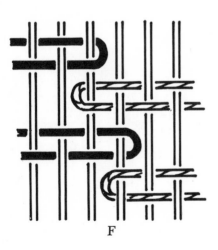

F

Outlining (Limning)

Outlining (or limning) a design was very much a part of Peruvian tapestry weaving. In some pieces, the background and figures are almost the same golden brown, and the black outline sets off the design. Several methods were used to accomplish this outlining. We describe just one of the methods of putting in a diagonal outline. It takes much planning and thinking ahead to keep the outline stepping up with the weaving on each side of it.

One way to outline on a diagonal

The outline weft is carried up as the adjacent rows are woven. It spirals up around a warp left empty when the pattern weft is returned, and follows the shape of the design being woven. To do it (3-29):

Weave from left to right: over two warps.

Weave from right to left: back under one warp.

Weave left to right; over two warps, and so on up.

FIGURE 3·29. Limning (Outlining). Method where outlining yarn spirals up between woven rows.

How to make a vertical outline

The outline weft is wound up the same warp as many times as needed for a straight line, then stepped over to follow a diagonal line.

FIGURE 3·30. Detail of Peruvian belt. Plain weave tapestry, design outlined. (Courtesy of Mrs. Charles Chapman.)

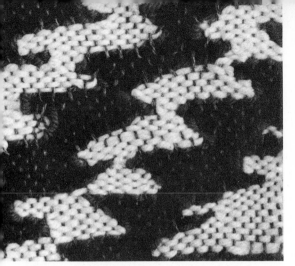

FIGURE 3-31. Turquoise wool outlines black wool pattern on white wool. Plain weave tapestry technique. (Adult student work. Courtesy of the Art Department, University of Washington. Richard M. Proctor, Instructor.)

HOW TO FORM WEFTS

Wefts can be manipulated into lozenge shapes, curves, undulating lines, or spots by modeling with a fork as beater, or with your fingers. The yarn can be pushed and crowded in to make a pointed end of a leaf, for instance, then more loosely beaten where the shape swells. This gives you great freedom of design, and permits many curving forms. See Figure 3-16 where the heads and eye-shapes were modeled in this manner.

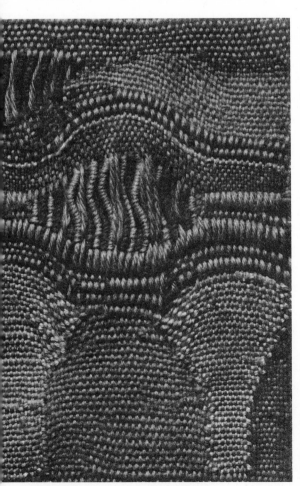

FIGURE 3-32. Weft curved and modeled. (Courtesy of the Museum of Modern Art, New York. Sheila Hicks, weaver.)

FIGURE 3-33. Space divider, woven hanging. Linen, rayon, mohair, saran, and jute. Natural, purple, and gold. (Courtesy of *Craft Horizons*, Mary Balzer Buskirk, weaver.)

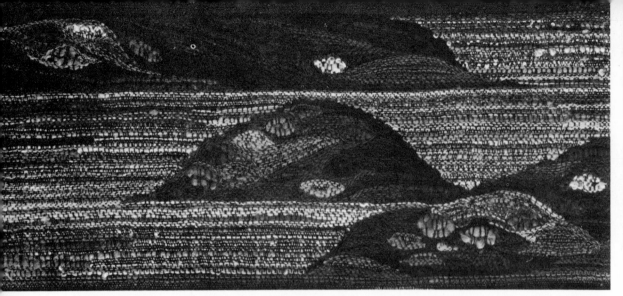

FIGURE 3-34.BAY. Rocky shore and islands, sparkling water. Freely applied tapestry techniques. Greens, grayish ground; warp of tweed wool. (Courtesy of the American Craftsman's Council. Collection of Mrs. Robert W. Bruce, Kentfield. Trude Guermonprez Elsesser, weaver.)

FIGURE 3-35. Adapted French, plain weave tapestry. Long slits sewn, small slits emphasize outlines. (Courtesy of Mrs. V. L. Georgeson, weaver.)

FIGURE 3-36. Swedish knot tapestry, woven on a simple frame and nail loom. Design is taken from a very old Quinalt Indian basket. Wool worsted. Dark brown, yellow, and gold tones suggest the colors used in the original basket. (Courtesy of the weaver, Gladys McIlveen, retired social worker with the United States Bureau of Indian Affairs.)

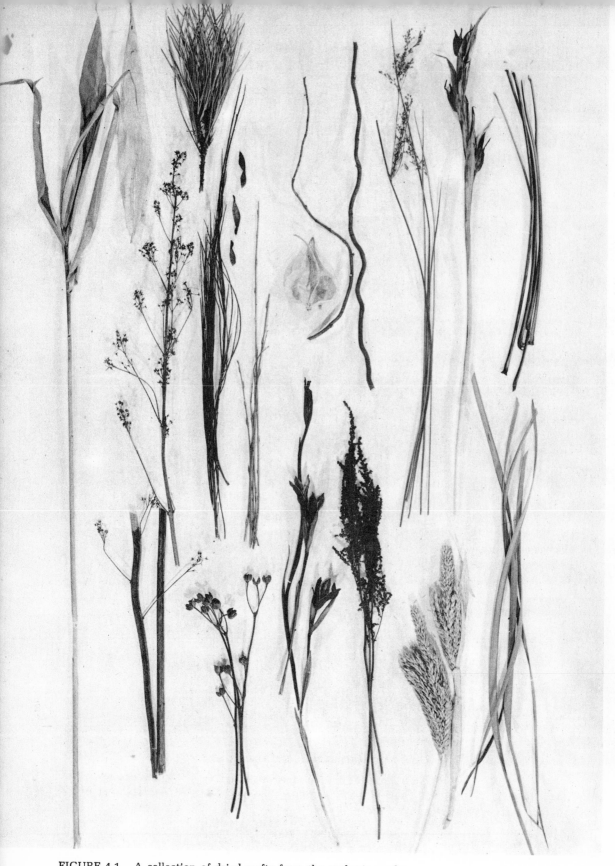

FIGURE 4-1 . A collection of dried wefts from the author's garden.

4 Weaving from Nature

AWARENESS

Develop the art of taking notice — of really seeing what is about you. Trust your eyes, instead of a rule or preconceived idea of what things ought to look like. You will make the most exciting discoveries. Tune your senses to respond to every harmony of line, color, form, and texture. When you attain the seeing eye you are well on your way to an understanding and enjoyment of the world around you. Because you will be aware of every little nuance of color, shade and shadow, form and construction, you will be a better designer and craftsman. Never before have we been able to see so much: for example, from high above we can perceive patterns on the earth made by rivers, lakes, oceans, roadways, farms, and forests. Powerful microscopes and cameras show us minute designs and thrilling colors. Just take time to walk in the woods, to study a dandelion, or to delight in the fiery red trail a water bird draws swimming by at sunrise. Follow the graceful swoops and loops of a swallow, filling the sky with an invisible line drawing. Or go to the kitchen and halve an apple! Study the satisfying design of seed and core. Life becomes rich and never boring, if you understand and appreciate what you see.

DESIGNING

We are all designers. We all have an inborn desire and need to create. Nothing else can give such a deep feeling of satisfaction. When you select materials and put them together, you are designing: whether it is putting together a beautiful salad, a perfect costume, a small flower arrangement, or a whole garden. When you want to weave a tweed fabric in woodsy colors, you are not likely to rush out and take a walk in the woods, but you will draw on your memory of the way the forest floor looks; the spongy feeling of the earth; the appearance of straight little pine needles combining with soft green moss and dots of yellow sunlight.

Bring into your designs inspired by nature not an imitation, but the gentle rhythms, a sense of underlying structure, and subtle color harmonies. You will have noticed that a repeated shape or line over a large area becomes a texture. Translate this into a rug. Look at the glowing yellow mushrooms in Figure C-16. They are texture, made up of smooth, rounded shapes, dull and shiny, grouped in an agreeably casual way, on a background of fine, rough-textured green with lights and shadows. Transferring this look into a woven fabric, you will not want the mushrooms actually standing up on stems. Abstract the design and weave a background of unevenly cut pile in shades of green ranging from light, bright, to dark; have the mushroom forms in sheared flat areas or in tightly packed loops, of yarn that is smoother than that of the grassy background. Just remember that you cannot weave the scent of a rose, or all of the rapidly changing colors in a sunset. Settle for the essence.

Translating ideas from nature can become a joyful game for a weaver. Decide which techniques will express a certain texture; or, conversely, let nature remind you of a weaving technique. Grass, of course, is cut pile. This is easy to see. A pussywillow is gray chenille, but if you are perceptive, you will find that the gray chenille should be woven on a yellow warp, with some dark brown wool and a little bit of off-white silk. A pebbled beach is a low-loop rug, but if you really look, you will see not only stone gray, but dozens of shades of grayed red, blue, green, and yellow. So weave your rug with several sizes of loops, several shades of gray, and some low-key blue and green. Get the idea? Before you know it, your discerning eye will be bringing you more design ideas for weaving than you will have time to fabricate. Our examples have been thoughtfully chosen for you to see. We hope to bring you some ideas —just enough to send you out on a rewarding hunt for more inspiration.

INSPIRATION FROM NATURE

Weavers are rediscovering the beauty in natural fibers and design elements found in early weaving. Primitive weavings are appealing because the materials used were natural. The fabrics created were those needed for a specific use. Man's inner need,

FIGURE 4-2. Very fine warp, almost invisibly holding meandering linen, seeds, and wood. (Courtesy of the American Craftsman's Council. Luella Williams, weaver.)

his appreciation and desire for beauty, caused him to make that material "pretty," to make it his very own distinctive creation. Without this desire and the basic talent to fulfill it, people would use only plain weave, in whatever fiber or material that could be put into a warp. Perfectly plain fabric will cover and give warmth, but cannot always satisfy our esthetic requirements.

Now, with so vast a supply of possible weaving material, from the most readily available grasses or reeds which you gather and dry for your own use, to a length of synthetic fiber or extruded plastic, the choice is yours. It is true that you can purchase woven fabrics of all kinds, ready to use; weaving does take time and thought and learning; it is also true that there is no substitute for creating. So, start on a project and see what you can do.

WEAVING WITH NATURAL MATERIALS

Almost any material that will hold still long enough to be put acros a warp and beaten in, is grist for a weaver! Although natural materials are a pleasure to weave, a large part of the enjoyment comes from selecting, gathering, and preparing the grasses and leaves you propose to use. This is really seeing nature; seeking something that will become a part of your woven piece, selecting colors and textures and being surprised at the number of suitable things you can find. Whether you go on a solitary search and follow through on your weaving alone, or make it a group enterprise with family or friends, your experience will be enriching.

A totally satisfying experience for the writer occurred while camping one summer on an island in the Pacific Northwest. First came the search for just the right pair of straight trees, growing just the right distance apart. Then there was a hunt for driftwood or branches to make the top and bottom beams of a primitive loom. When

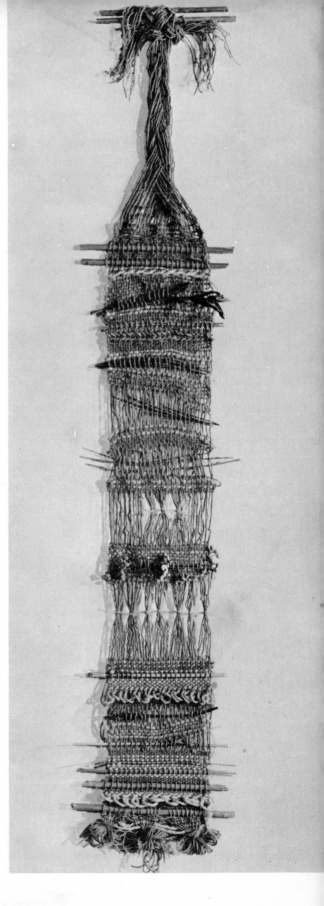

FIGURE 4-3. Tansy, iris, bracken, and broom. Wall hanging by the author.

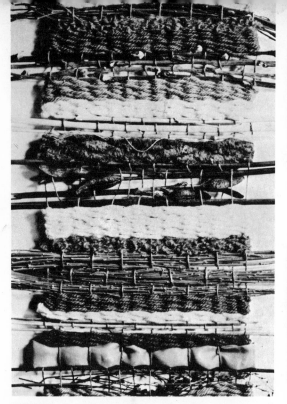

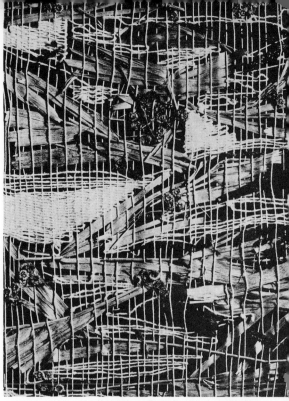

FIGURE 4-4. Pussywillow, chenille, stems, and wool. (Courtesy of the Sammamish High School Art Class. Photograph by Clydene Phelps.)

FIGURE 4-5. A dynamic mixture of dried material and woven string. (Courtesy of Sammamish High School Art Class. Photograph by Clydene Phelps.)

these were slung and secured between the trees, a warp of cotton string in soft brown and dull orange was put on. Then came the fun of searching for weaving materials. Bracken fern stems, dried, firm, rich golden brown from last year's growth were still standing, waiting to be picked. The trees bore lacy strands of moss — a lovely gray-green. At the edge of the water were some clumps of reeds, some green, some dried and brown. These, with an occasional row of the string, were woven into an open, airy wall hanging. A piece of driftwood served as a shuttle; a cut of a log-end was a stool. This was an experience of complete weaving from nature, including the outdoor weaving with sea gulls and fishing boats to watch between throws of the shuttle.

You can capture a part of this rapport with nature, just by weaving with dried growing things. Some critics are amused at what weavers do with natural materials.

These fanciful weavings are play; they are not always made to be taken too seriously. Some are quite fragile. They are not woven for the ages, but are made, perhaps for a single occasion, or with the full knowledge that they may not last very long. Others are surprisingly hardy. Mats and blinds of bamboo, bark, or reeds are very practical and long-lived.

NATURE'S WEFTS

Nature presents us with an almost endless variety of wefts. A recent walk through my yard yielded more than a dozen: pine needles, bracken, sedge, bamboo, iris, water iris, willow branches, horsetails, scotch broom, and more. All of these are suitable: straw, wheat, reeds, teasel stalks, tall grasses, raffia, palm leaves, banana fiber, cedar bark, iris leaves, goldenrod stems, sisal, pampas, yucca, moss, lichen, honey-

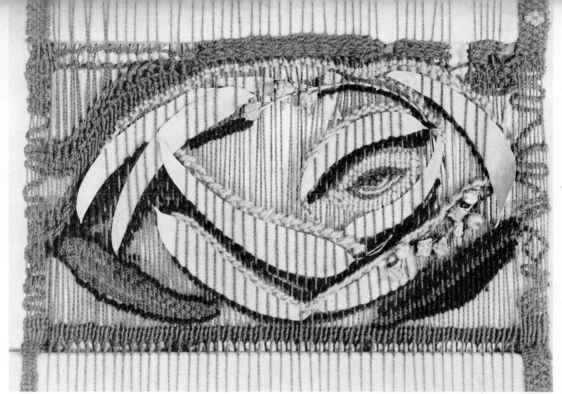

FIGURE 4-6. EUCALYPTUS. Pods, stems, and leaves. A memento of a pleasant trip to California, woven into a wall picture. Wool warp and weft: deep gray-blue; and the leaves: dusty gray-green. Left on frame to keep it in tension. Woven by the author.

suckle vine, corn husks, swamp grasses, tules, cattails, eucalyptus leaves and stems, pods. Almost any kind of vine, leaf, stem, or stalk is usable, if it is not too bulky or brittle when dried. One especially beautiful branch or seed pod can be the focal point or feature of a wall hanging, or the whole piece can be woven with rows of stems and fibers.

How to prepare and use Nature's wefts

Long stems and leaves should be dried reasonably straight and flat. One method is to tie them to a broom handle or narrow flat board. Preserve any natural kinks and curves, as they may set the line for your whole design. The more brittle leaves and flat grasses may be slightly dampened before weaving to make them easier to han-

dle. You may weave with freshly picked material, but you must be prepared for a certain amount of shrinkage and change of color or shade when it dries. For example, bamboo leaves are green when fresh, but dry to a soft golden beige. If you are in doubt about how certain things will work out, experiment. Dry them; try them!

Jointed grasses, prevalent in damp environments are a lovely deep gray-green when dried, with a gray and black stripe at each joint. Gently pressed to flatten them before they are fully dried, they weave up into an unusual mat sturdy enough to be used time and again with pottery or stoneware dishes. As time passes, some of them become a green-gold, but in nature's way of blending colors, they are still harmonious.

FIGURE 4-7. Mats or blinds of natural wefts. Left: Bamboo leaves and stems, soft gold cotton ratine yarn and unspun wool vegetable-dyed gray-green. Right (top): Bundles of long pine needles, crisp gray-green tree moss. Right (bottom): Jointed grass. Off-white warp echoes the stripe at the joint. Woven by the author.

WARPS TO USE WITH DRIED MATERIALS

Your warp should be kept in proportion to the scale of the weft you are using. For instance, a fairly fine reed or narrow length of iris leaf should be woven into a warp not much coarser than carpet warp. Bracken or cattail stems are best in a warp of jute or heavy cotton. Doubled or tripled carpet warp may be used with thick stems or bundles of reeds. The warp sett should also be in proportion to the size of the weft. Remember that the weft is the important part of this kind of weaving. As few as four warp threads to the inch when you use long lengths of weft will show it off to best advantage. For a mat which will get hard wear and more handling than a wall hanging, a closer sett is advisable. For example, the weft of small bundles of pine needles (the ones that are at least 5 inches long) requires six or eight warp threads to the inch. Allow plenty of length in the warp. Round stems like cattails can take up several extra inches in half a yard.

FIGURE 4-8. Window blinds woven with strips of split cedar, which has the soft sheen of satin; strings of orange wooden beads and widely spaced groups of textured warp threads. (Courtesy of Hella Skowronski, weaver. Photograph by Don Normark.)

Warp color

The color of the warp is also very important. A blended, neutral, inconspicuous warp in a grayed tone is a much better choice than a warp with a harsh, bright color. Your weft is featured. The warp is just the medium to hold it together. A soft yellow warp will suggest sunshine; a brown or green one, shadows; a muted blue one, sky or water.

Finishing

You can spray the finished weaving with a preservative spray which will retard the change of color with further drying. However, it is wise to experiment on unwoven samples to see if the spray changes the color or surface. You would not want to destroy the whole natural look and patina by having a shiny or varnished-looking result.

4-10

FIGURE 4-9. Stems, bunched and woven in varied widths, and one fascinating row woven with threads unravelled from burlap, brought out between warps and twisted to form a burst of loops. (Courtesy of the Sammamish High School Art Class. Photograph by Clydene Phelps.)

FIGURES 4-10, 11. Two studies by students aged 17, Lincoln High School, Portland, Oregon. The problem: to demonstrate the concept of weaving; to show how man began weaving; to start the search for materials other than threads. 4-10, Iris leaves, flat and straight; lamb's-ear leaves, soft and wooly. 4-11, Fine, bushy flower heads dried to a rich red-brown, tied to chunky sticks with dull red gift wrap ribbon.

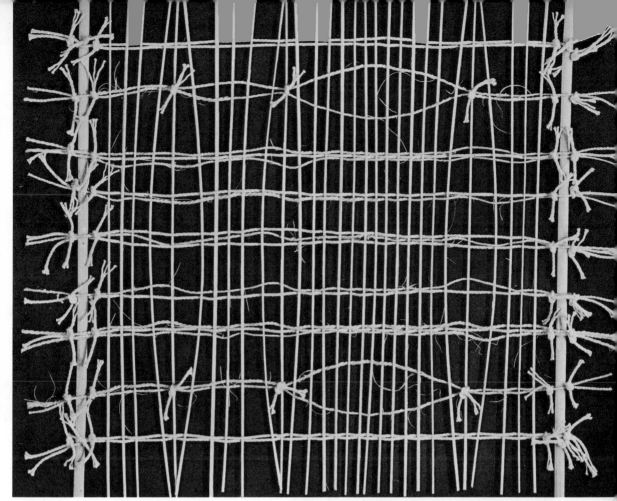

FIGURE 4-12. Very fine bamboo, lemon yellow; sisal twine, orange. Plain weave and knots strategically placed. (Adult student work. Courtesy of the Art Department, University of Washington. Richard M. Proctor, Instructor.)

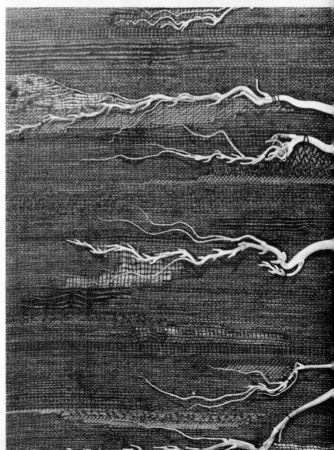

FIGURE 4-13. Royal palm fruit branches woven in against a background of warm browns, golds, orange, and yellow. Cotton, ramie, rayon, and vegetable-dyed wools. Notice how different wefts are skillfully woven into and around the convolutions of the branches. (Courtesy of Jean J. Williams, weaver. Photograph by Thelma Warner.)

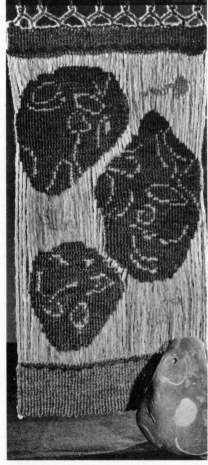

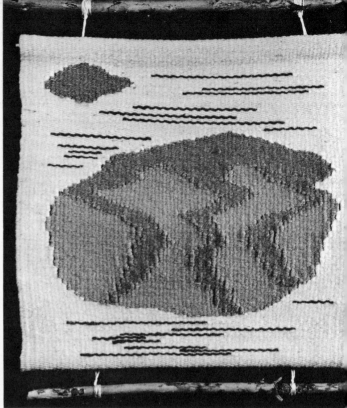

FIGURE 4-15 THE BEACH. Design and colors suggest sand, water, pebbles. Plain weave tapestry, slits used as part of the design. Wool, natural white, and vegetable dyed. (Courtesy of W. Ron Crosier, weaver.)

FIGURE 4-14. Design from the beach. A fossil stone with shells embedded inspired this appealing little wall hanging. The woven areas are done in Swedish knot tapestry technique. Made on a small frame with nails to hold the warp. A crocheted chain stitch twists along the top on a smooth, painted dowel. Warp and weft two shades of stone gray worsted. Three small woven spots are light green. (Courtesy of Gladys McIlveen, weaver.)

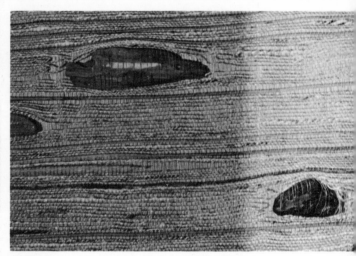

FIGURE 4-16. Detail of a semisheer wall hanging. A combination of rayon, wool, and linen yarns in natural and grayed tones. Casually spaced rows of salt-water rush, and caged bits of driftwood and water-smoothed bark create interest in this plain weave. Observe how pockets are formed for the wood by weaving up to and around them. (Courtesy of Juanita Minard, weaver. Photograph by Fortescue.)

FIGURE 4-17. A design project from a sand dollar found on a Pacific beach. The design was worked out on squared paper, revised, painted with poster paints, then woven in Swedish knot tapestry technique. Woven on a small frame, none of the remaining warp was cut, but knotted at the last row of weaving, then gathered at the top into a knot to hang it by. (Courtesy of Gladys McIlveen, weaver.)

FIGURE 4-18 AURORA. Vibrant
reds and yellows. Gobelin tapestry
technique. (Courtesy of W. Ron
Crosier, weaver.)

5 Color

Color experience in weaving differs from that in any other medium. Something happens to colors in yarns when they are brought together and interlaced that is unlike what happens when paints or woven fabrics are combined. Color studies must be amplified and confirmed by actual samplings, to find out just what does occur when colors are interwoven. Each color borrows from, modifies, or intensifies the other. Size, texture, brilliance, juxtaposition, and weaving plan all play a part in the total effect.

CHOOSING YARNS

Two or more values of one color will produce a fabric with much more interest and life than exact matches. For example, choose a warp of medium gray. For the weft have alternate rows of slightly lighter and a little darker gray than the warp. A third color is achieved by weaving with two other colors. Yellow warp and gray-blue weft result in a yellow-green fabric with a lively look, more pleasing than a warp and weft dyed to the exact shade of yellow-green you desire. For example, a necktie was wanted in a vibrant blue-green or turquoise shade. A warp of purple-blue, crossed with a weft of green-blue resulted in blue-green fabric with depth and life.

To achieve a fabric in a grayed or sub-dued color, weave with yarns of opposing hues. The balance is tipped to the color of the yarn the heaviest in weight, the brightest in color, or the most often used. Half of a coarse green yarn and half of a fine red yarn will produce a fabric of a toned-down green.

COLOR STUDY PROJECT

A color blanket, which is a useful color study, is also fascinating to weave. If you enjoy picturesque names, call your color blanket a "gamp." The story goes that weavers named gamps after Dickens' Sairey Gamp and her ever-present, large, untidy umbrella with a colored patch. Perhaps this was because of the umbrella of leaf brown and blue, or because of Sairey Gamp's colorful character — or both! The color blanket is made of woven squares of color; the warp is of stripes of solid color. Since the weft is woven in the same color sequence, each color is crossed by itself and by all of the others. Using only eight colors, for instance, you will have a gamp showing 64 combinations. On one diagonal, you will have squares of pure color. All other squares will be combinations of colors. Two quite different examples show results obtained with a very fine mercerized cotton and wool knitting worsted (C-8).

Size and colors

Ideally, a gamp should be about 36 inches square, with each color square about 2 inches. However, studies made on a small frame will be quite helpful, especially to a beginning weaver.

A simple version is to use carpet warp, mercerized cotton or wool worsted, in the six basic color wheel hues: purple, blue, green, yellow, orange, red, plus black and white. Part of the value of the experience is that the weaver chooses colors and combinations and decides on whether to use muted, bright, or light hues. The only rule to go by in making a color blanket is that each color used in the warp must be crossed by an equal measure of its own color, and all of the other colors, in the same order, warp and weft. All colors used should be of the same intensity.

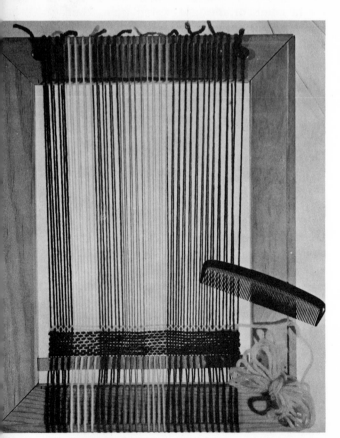

FIGURE 5-1. Warp on frame ready to weave color blanket. Woven by the author.

When you progress to a floor loom, each square can be threaded to a different pattern. Since many hues and values can be used, it will be a pattern and color blanket with an infinite number of combinations. Add to these a variety of weights and textures, and your color blanket becomes a whole color text.

If you prefer, you can make several color studies on small frames, only two or three colors each. This might be a good idea for a class project, with each student working with only one small group of colors. For example, weave blue, blue-green, and green together; or red, orange, and yellow; or try one with three or six colors, and weave them with gray, black, and white.

How to weave a small color blanket

Please read the section on Warping in Chapter 6 and on Frames in Chapter 2. For our example we used a canvas stretcher frame and wool knitting yarn, eight threads to the inch, and six colors: purple, blue, green, yellow, orange, red — black, and white.

You will need

> Frame (Ours: 8½ by 11½ inches, inside measurement).
> Warp: wool worsted, mercerized cotton or carpet warp. Colors, black and white.
> Weft: exactly the same as the warp.
> Comb for a beater.
> ½ inch strip of cardboard, about 8¼ inches long.
> Two thumbtacks.
> Pencil, ruler, scissors.

How to warp

Make a mark at the top of the frame, ¼ inch in from the inside corner of the frame. Measure and mark every inch across to the other side. Repeat at the opposite end of the frame. Make sure that the marks all line up exactly across from each other so that the warp will be straight. Each color will make four complete turns around the frame; there will be eight warp threads in each inch. It is a good idea to measure off the amount you will need of each color and wind it into a little ball. Place these beside you in the proper sequence to keep from having to stop and prepare the next color of warp. Knot the first warp thread around the frame, or tie it around a thumbtack, as we did. To keep the warp tension while you tie the next color warp on, use the other thumbtack to hold the end of the first warp color fast to the frame. Always

tie on at the top, outside edge of the frame. Space the warp threads equally between the inch marks, eight in each inch. Wind the warp on in figure 8. Tie the last warp around the frame or thumbtack. Now you are ready to weave.

How to weave

Slip the 1/2-inch strip of cardboard into the shed made by the figure 8, push and pull down to the bottom of the frame. The first warp color on the left is purple, so

FIGURE 5-2. Finished color blanket. Even in black and white, you can see the gradations of color. From left, colors are: purple, blue, green, yellow, orange, red, white, black. Woven by the author.

make a butterfly of purple weft, weave over and under across the warp, turning in the end of weft, weave over and under two or three warps to secure it. To avoid having to add in extra weft length of any one color, wind enough in your butterfly to go ten or twelve times across the warp, plus about 2 inches for tuck-ins at the ends. It is quite important to beat the weft in as evenly as possible. After you weave a few rows, measure the width of each strip, then weave enough rows of each color to square up. Check the beating to be sure you are not pressing the weft in too tightly. The rows should just touch, so that the warp colors will show. Your next color will be blue. Repeat this same procedure for each row of color. When you finish the last row at the top, which will be black, weave in a few extra rows as a weft protector, to keep the weft from unravelling when you cut the gamp from the loom. We finished the edge with knotting and a row of overcast stitching. The overcast stitch, or blanket or chain stitch can be done before removing the fabric from the loom.

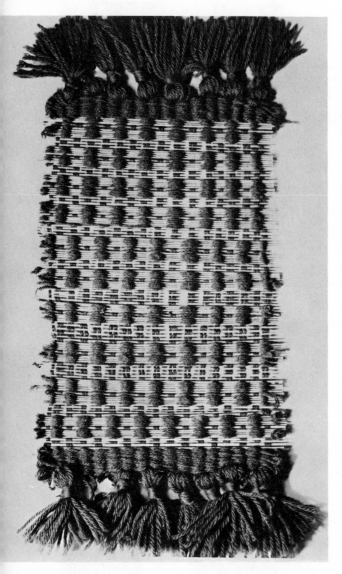

FIGURE 5-3. Pattern in plain weave; rug yarn and fine swamp reeds contrast color and size. (Courtesy of the Sammamish High School Art Class. Photograph by Clydene Phelps.)

6 What to Weave

WEAVING PROJECTS FOR YOUNG HANDS

Young weavers may be intrigued by rugs for dollhouses, doll blankets, a small Navaho rug, a saddle blanket, book covers, place mats, fancy pockets for dresses or skirts, a ski belt with purse attached for handkerchiefs and keys, doll clothes, headbands, small curtains for playhouse or dollhouse, tote bags, shoe bags, small aprons, little quilts, knee robes or afghans, wall hangings, and tapestries from their own drawings.

For quick weaving, you can make sturdy mats for floor or table — colorful, useful, and handsome. Use jute for warp, and weave alternate rows of jute and folded burlap. Weave round mats on a wheel loom. For a Christmas door decoration, have a warp of green jute, only 1 inch wide. Weave in graduated strips of green florist sticks to make a Christmas tree triangle shape. Weave short sticks at the bottom for a tub shape. Warp up the middle is a tree trunk. Weave the jute about 2 inches above the tip of the tree as a hanging strip. Remove from the loom and hang miniature ornaments at the ends of the "branches," and a little star at the top. For a Fall party, weave place mats of dried iris leaves, long pine needles, bracken fern stems, cornhusks, or whatever dried material is at hand. The warp can be jute or coarse cotton, set only about six warps to the inch. The weaving will not take much more time than going to town for paper mats, and of course is a lot more imaginative.

For a gift, weave a set of round coasters on a round cardboard loom. Use heavy rug cotton or jute or a synthetic yarn, in one or two gay colors. On a larger size round cardboard loom weave a reversible hot-dish mat. Weave on both sides, and each side can be a different color.

For eye-glasses, weave a firm wool or cotton case. Weave a little wider than twice the width needed, to allow for seam and thickness of folded glasses. Sew together and all round the edge with a decorative stitch. Allow enough length to turn in a hem at the top.

Weave a pretty collar for your dog or cat out of strips of leather or plastic, or yarn of any kind or color. Leave long warp ends to braid and tie, or fasten with a buckle.

As a gift for a flower arranger, weave a special mat to complement her favorite flower bowl. Do not have too busy a design, though, which would compete with the flowers. For a bride, gay fingertip or guest towels make very successful woven gifts.

SIZE CHART

Here is a guide to standard sizes of some of the articles you might choose to weave.

Afghans, small lap robes or knee robes, of units joined together: 54 by 72 inches, 38 by 48 inches, 30 by 40 inches.

Baby bibs: Size of baby!

Crib blankets: 40 by 60 inches, 36 by 50 inches, 30 by 42 inches (carriage), 38 by 38 inches (shawl).

Bath mats: 22 by 34 inches, 24 by 36 inches.

Cocktail napkins: 5 by 8 inches.

Table mats: Suitable size for your dishes and table; 14 by 21 inches, 12 by 18 inches.

Napkins: 12 by 12 inches, 14 by 14 inches — or your choice.

Fingertip towels: 8 by 16 inches.

Rugs: Size of the space you want to cover. Some usual proportions: 3 by 5 feet, 4 by 6 feet, 5 by 7 feet.

Mats to be used under flower arrangements, treasures, or on trays, should be sized for your special use.

Tapestries and wall hangings can be woven in pleasing proportion and size suitable to use and setting.

YOU CAN WEAVE THESE ON SIMPLE LOOMS

ITEM	TECHNIQUES	YARNS
Rugs, bath mats, sit-upon mats, floor pillows, cushions. (Size limited to size of frame or vertical loom. Several small rugs can be joined to make larger sizes.)	Flat or plain weave Knots, loops Navaho, Kilim, Soumak Twining, chaining	Wool Cotton Jute Cloth strips, wool, cotton, burlap
Tapestries, wall hangings. (Size limited to frame; small ones joined or planned as parts of a group hung together.)	Plain weave or tapestry knot Knots, loops Wrapped weaves Needle stitches Plain weave Combinations of all	Unlimited possibilities. Wool, cotton, Natural fibers, dried material, silk, synthetics
Place mats, runners Tablecloths in strips or squares	Plain weave Borders, stripes, plaids, checks Spots laid-in, Needle stitches	Linen, cotton Ramie Synthetics Jute Dried material
Scarves, stoles, jackets, pullovers Baby sweaters	See above, place mats	Wool, orlon Mohair Linen, cotton
Belts, dog collars, hatbands	See above, place mats Simple patterns in tapestry weaves	Wool, cotton Jute Leather or plastic strips
Afghans, knee robes, baby blankets	Plain weave, borders Spots of tapestry weave	Wool, orlon Mohair

IDEA PAGES

Here are some more ideas for you: other things to weave, and ways to weave them on other types of looms. The following looms are a little different, fun to know about, and maybe to try.

One of the earliest looms could have been the warp-weighted loom. Warps are tied around a branch. Then stones are tied to weight the warp and put it under some tension (6-1). A next logical step is the use of a stick for a bottom beam, with just a few weights (6-2).

The Indians of the Amazon jungle make bead aprons on a bow loom. A green willow branch is bent into a U shape, a stick lashed across the bottom (6-3). Why not try one yourself, and weave a little apron? Three lengths of warp are stretched and tied near the top, with ends long enough to braid for the waist ties. Weave from the top down.

Weave a belt, with the buckle for the loom (6-4). Loop the doubled warp over one edge of the buckle and fingerweave a belt. If you want to put on tension, tie the warp between two chairs.

To weave a square for a rug with fringe all around, a rug unit, or units for a coverlet, make a loom out of an old card table. Remove the top, leaving the frame and legs (6-5). The warp can be wound around and around, or in a figure 8 warp, or if the frame is wood, nails pounded in to hold the warp. If two legs are folded back, you will have an easel-type upright loom.

FIGURE 6-3. Bow loom.

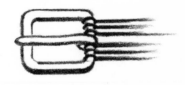

FIGURE 6-4. Weave a belt.

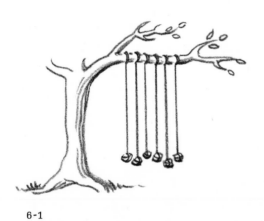

6-1

FIGURES 6-1, 2. Warp-weighted looms.

FIGURE 6-5. Card table loom.

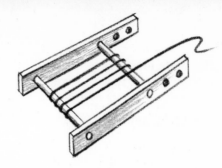

To make an expandable frame loom, use boards and dowels for the frame (6-6). Bore a series of holes so that the dowel can be moved to make different lengths for weaving space. If you want to put your loom on a slant, fasten movable legs to your frame loom with wing nut and bolt (6-7).

FIGURE 6-6. Expandable frame loom.

The following can be woven to shape on a board loom: a triangular scarf, with all edges finished; segment of a circle for a handbag, or place mats for a round table; a baby jacket or sweater. For the front of the jacket, with opening, weave left and right sides around the nails. For the back, remove the two center rows of nails and weave across in one piece. For a pullover, weave both front and back the same.

FIGURE 6-7. Loom put on a slant.

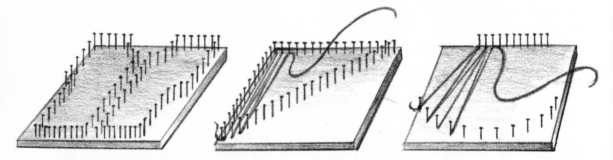

FIGURE 6-8. Three looms for weaving shaped articles.

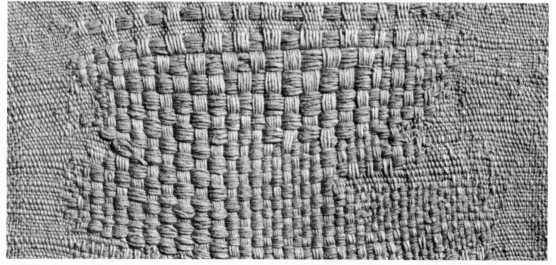

FIGURE 6-9. Variation on a plain weave theme. (Courtesy of Sheila Hicks, weaver, and *Handweaver & Craftsman*. Photograph by Ferdinand Boesch.)

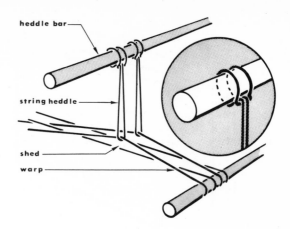

FIGURE 6-10. String heddles.

WARPING, HEDDLES, AND SHED

The warp is the stretched thread fastened to the loom, the foundation you weave upon. The heddles are warp lifters; the shed is the space opened by the raised heddles so that the weft yarn can be put through. In this text we are concerned only with simple ways to put short warps on simple looms. For now, you will need to know only these methods of warping for the looms included. We refer you to the Bibliography for many fine books on weaving, most of which have very good sections on ways to make long warps.

Two kinds of warping are the continuous warp and figure 8 warp. By continuous warp, we mean a warp that is not pre-measured, but that is wound directly onto the loom from the spool. A figure 8 warp is a continuous warp wound in a figure 8 around a frame.

Heddles

Because each row of plain weaving requires the weft to be taken over and under every warp thread, it saves a great deal of time and tedious picking up of each individual warp thread to install some kind of a warp-lifting device to lift alternate warp threads all at once. Heddles are warp lifters, attached to a heddle bar, which is lifted by hand to open the shed (6-10). String heddles can be used on any kind of loom needing such a device: frames, board looms, vertical, backstrap, or round looms.

A common way to form string heddles is to loop the heddle string over the heddle bar, and around the warp threads, with one continuous length. This method, used particularly on primitive looms, is shown on the backstrap loom in our Project section; and on the Mexican loom (2-41).Individual heddles can be tied, looped on the heddle bar, and the alternate warp threads put through them, as seen in Figure 6-11. These are just two of the ways possible.

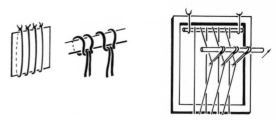

FIGURE 6-11. How to make and install string heddles.

Shed

One set of heddles will lift just one set of warp threads. For the second shed, the weaving sword (shed sword, shed stick) is used to pick up the other warp threads. The weaving sword is a flat, smooth stick, tapered at one or both ends. To open the second shed, the sword is turned on edge.

As weaving patterns become more complex, more rows of heddles can be added to lift up pattern warp threads. Upright tapestry looms seem to be festooned with string heddles which are pulled by hand in small bunches, wherever an area of pattern is put in and a small shed is needed. One shed is automatically formed in a figure 8 warp. The second shed is made by weaving in the shed stick.

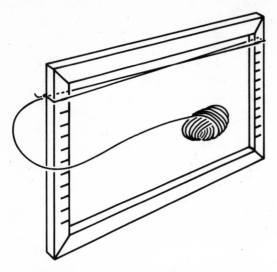

FIGURE 6-12. How to put on a figure 8 warp.

FIGURE 6-13. Cross section, figure 8 warp.

Warping

To make a figure 8 warp

To put a figure 8 warp on a frame, first measure and mark along the top and bottom of the frame where the warp threads will be so that you will put on the right number per inch, evenly spaced. Start the warp at least 2 inches in, inside of the frame, to leave working room on each side of the warp.

As an example, for eight threads to the inch, mark each ¼ inch across the width of the frame. Four warps in each inch are at the back of the frame, four on the front. The first thread of each new inch will be on the inch mark. Wind a ball of weft, a comfortable size to handle. If necessary, you can tie on more, always being careful to put the knot out on the frame, not in the weaving space. Tie the end of the warp around the frame at the first mark. Pull it tightly, keep tension as even as possible, and carry the ball of warp to the other end of the frame, over, around, back of the frame, and down to the other end. Go down, around and over, up to the top again, making a figure 8. See Figure 6-13. A cross

will be formed in the center of the frame where the threads pass each other. Check frequently to make sure you are going over and under each time. Put a warp thread on each mark, all across to the last mark. The tension of the warp should be as even as possible, but relaxed enough so that you can stretch it a little to put the weft through. Tie the end around the frame twice, in a double knot.

Check once again for errors. You will be able to see a thread out of line instantly. To flatten and even out the warp, weave in two or three rows of warp thread at the bottom of the frame for a heading, as follows: measure off a length of warp thread about four and a half times the width of the loom. Tie one end around the frame on the right. Look through the warp sideways and you will see where the cross comes in the figure 8. Put this weft thread through the top part of the figure 8, for this is the shed that is made automatically in the figure 8. As it will be a little hard to beat down to the bottom of the frame, ease it down about 1 inch at a time, using a fork for a beater. Beat in evenly. Pull through and wind the end around the frame twice, return the weft to the other side by weaving over and under. Do not take this row around the frame, but weave it in over to the other side. Cut, turn the end in over two or three warp threads to secure it. Beat evenly all the way across. This is your heading. Two or three rows can be woven across the top of the frame in the same manner, with one row being tied around the frame at each end. (To warp a backstrap loom, see Chapter 8.)

To put a warp around pins or nails

For this type of warping, put the warp around each pin separately, as shown in our drawings; or if wider spacing is wanted or coarse yarn is being used, put the warp around two pins, then down to the other end, around two, and so on.

To loop warp around a bar

Learning to loop a double warp thread over a bar like this will prove useful in many different situations. It is one way to fasten the warp to the warp beam on a backstrap loom. If you want the warp or cloth beam to be your hanger for a wall hanging, you can put the warp on your hanger this way. Also, when a belt buckle or ring is to serve as your warp beam, loop the warp on like this. Separate, single loop string heddles are put over the heddle stick in this fashion.

How to do it: cut the warp threads two times as long as you need for your weaving. Be sure to add extra inches for the take-up of thread going around the bar and tying on at the other end. Double each length and loop over the bar as in Figure 6-14.

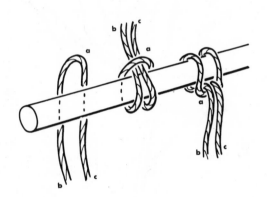

FIGURE 6-14. How to loop a double warp thread over a bar.

To estimate the amount of warp

How to estimate the amount of warp: for a figure 8 warp on a frame, measure the length of your frame from top to bottom, add in the thickness of the top frame (only). This will give you the length of one warp thread. Multiply this by the number of warps per inch. Then multiply that total by the width of the warp for the total inches of warp you will need. Divide by 36 to find out the number of yards of warp. Add on 12 inches for tying around frame at beginning and end. For a loom with pins or nails, measure the distance between top and bottom pin for length of one warp. Always add on at least 3 inches for tying at beginning and end.

HELPFUL WEAVING NOTES FOR ANY SIZE LOOM

How to begin and end the weft

Turn the end of the weft around the outside warp thread, weave in, over, and under at least three warps. The weft may be trimmed off after a few rows have been woven beyond (6-15). Never leave a cut end of weft at the selvage. Always be sure it turns back in. If you are using several weft yarns in the same row, bring the ends up between successive warps to cut so that there will not be a bump where they all end at the same spot.

FIGURE 6-15. How to secure beginning and ending of weft.

How to have straight selvages

The edges, or selvages (selvedges) of cloth are a very important part of your weaving, and should be done with care. On a rug, place mat, or other woven piece where edges will be left as woven, it is of prime importance to have a straight, neatly woven selvage. When you return the weft around the edge, be sure it is relaxed enough not to pull the outside warp in, but not so loose that it loops. Putting the weft through at an angle, or slight arc, will al-

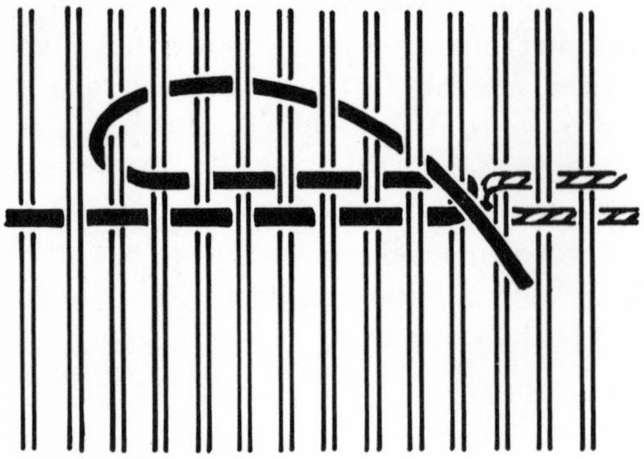

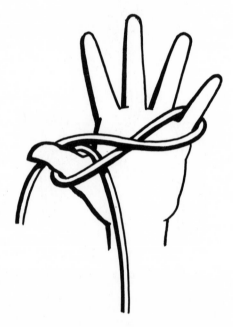

FIGURE 6-16. Bubbling or arc.

Bobbins

Bobbins are also used for small lengths of weft in small spaces. Weft can be wound on a piece of cardboard, small cylinder of paper, or a small flat ball wound around two fingers. The reel or spool holding the weft yarn to put into a shuttle is also called a bobbin. See the Illustrated Definitions in Chapter 1 for sketches of a few kinds of bobbins and shuttles.

low plenty of yarn to beat in without having it draw at the edge. This is called "bubbling," or "arcing," (6-16). A stiff wire is sometimes put in at each side of a frame loom. The weft is carried around it and the outside warp, as one. See the Lilette Loom, in Chapter 2.

Butterflies

Weavers are inventive, as are all craftsmen. Tools and methods are developed by the people doing the work. Since wefts must be taken across the warp, the weaver will suit the tool or method to the work. When a shuttle is too large or too stiff to use, make a butterfly. This is a soft bundle of yarn wound in such a way that the end feeds out of the center. See Figures 6-17 and 6-18.

FIGURE 6-17. How to make a butterfly.

To make a butterfly, loop yarn around thumb, and let an end of several inches hang down over your palm. Carry yarn around the little finger, over and around thumb, in a figure 8. Wind back and forth until you have a few yards, remove from hand, wind several times around the center. Cut the end and tuck in securely. The long end coming from the center is the working end.

FIGURE 6-18. Butterfly bobbin.

Two ways to sew strips or units of weaving together

Figure 6-19 shows two joining stitches that are especially suitable when you want the two edges of fabric to just meet, but not overlap: for example, when sewing squares together for an afghan. However, these stitches will also work well if you put one edge of the fabric slightly over the other and sew the two together. Place your stitches as close together as necessary to get a firm joining. The drawings are expanded to show more clearly how the stitches are made.

FIGURE 6-19, A and B. A, Ball or baseball stitch. Sew the two pieces of fabric together at the edge, with an overcast stitch, then follow the numbers. The thread is passed from one side to the other. B, Cross-stitch joining. Sew together at the very edge with an overcast stitch, then follow the arrows and numbers. The stitch passes from edge to edge, with a cross on top.

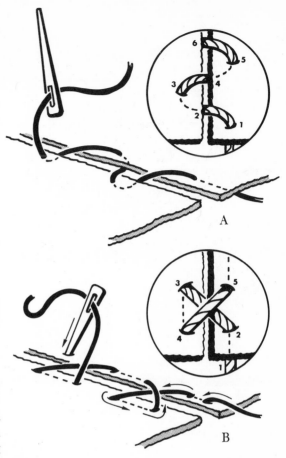

A

B

Finger weaving

This is a kind of plaiting or braiding done without using a loom. A group of warp threads are knotted together, hung over a nail or hook, and the warps interlaced in different combinations. A good sampling idea to find combinations of yarns and colors.

FIGURE 6-20. These are examples of finger weaving. A study in using a variety of materials, i.e., jute, wool, kraft cord, butcher twine, lace, mohair, nylon hose strips, seine twine. (Adult student work. Courtesy of the Art Department, University of Washington. Richard M. Proctor, Instructor.)

FIGURE 7-1. Collage of handwoven fabrics. Background is dark and light green nubby cotton uphol-stery fabric, handwoven. Patches are in shades of blue, blue-green, yellow-green, and gray-green. Black needlework lines. Woven by the author.

7 Small Weavings

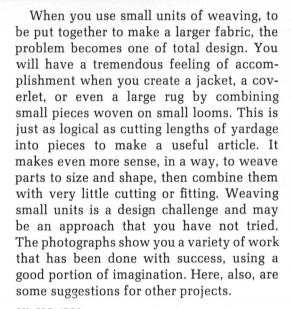

When you use small units of weaving, to be put together to make a larger fabric, the problem becomes one of total design. You will have a tremendous feeling of accomplishment when you create a jacket, a coverlet, or even a large rug by combining small pieces woven on small looms. This is just as logical as cutting lengths of yardage into pieces to make a useful article. It makes even more sense, in a way, to weave parts to size and shape, then combine them with very little cutting or fitting. Weaving small units is a design challenge and may be an approach that you have not tried. The photographs show you a variety of work that has been done with success, using a good portion of imagination. Here, also, are some suggestions for other projects.

AN OLD IDEA

Of course the whole idea of using narrow strips or small squares to create a garment or covering is not a new one. A study of early Egyptian, Peruvian, African, Indian — almost any culture — will yield a wealth of information on the use of small weavings to make large textiles. Simple looms and frames with little or no provision for a long warp; width limited by the convenient reach of the weaver, or available weft materials; or limitations in the design of the loom, all these influenced the style of clothing, accessories, and household textiles.

WEAVING IN UNITS
How to weave a rug in units

Remember the old woven rag-rug strips sewn together? Rug units lend themselves very well to joining. Create an accent rug or one to cover a large area. A combination of flat weave and loops or cut pile can be designed so the joining seams will be covered with the nap, and your rug will look just like one made on a wide warp, in one piece. All of the following must be very carefully studied: choice of weaving frame, yarns, weaving method, joining technique, and the size of the space to be filled.

Where to start

First measure the space you want to cover. Then figure out how your overall size breaks down into workable unit sizes. Decide if you want an all-pile, partly flat weave, or an all flat-weave rug.

Designing the rug

Now work out your design, keeping in mind the techniques, where it must be joined, and the kind of yarn you wish to use. Figure 7-2 shows one section of a rug planned to be woven in three sections and sewn together under the knotted, cut pile. The center section, part of which is shown, is nearly all flat weave with just a few rows of knotted cut pile. This joins the third section, which is all cut pile. Several

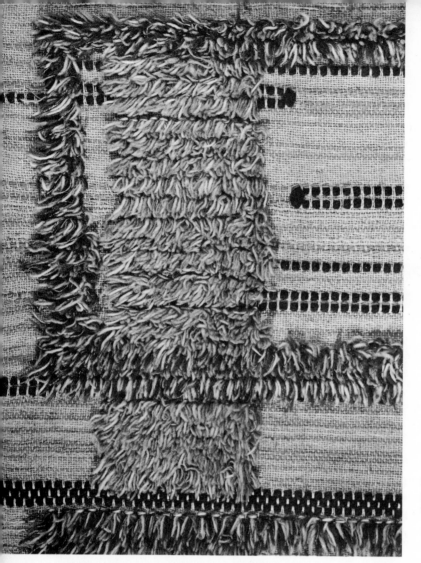

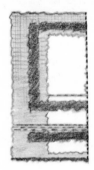

FIGURE 7-2. Woven section of rug shown in sketches below. By the author.

FIGURE 7-3. One third of the whole rug design, used in the woven section shown.

rows of heavy, dark yarn are run in and out to carry these horizontal lines throughout the whole composition (7-4). The same idea can be scaled up or down — perhaps using six units, each about 14 inches by 30 inches joined to make a rug about 3 feet by 5 feet. This would require a weaving frame with inside measurements of about 18 inches by 36 inches, to allow for working space within the frame, hems, and take-up in the weaving. If your design is all cut pile there is no particular design problem because none of the joinings will show and your units can be any size convenient for you. Rush and grass matting squares from Tahiti and the Philippines also utilize the idea of sewing squares together. The old patchwork quilt system again!

FIGURE 7-4. Rug designed to be woven in sections. Joining hidden by pile knots.

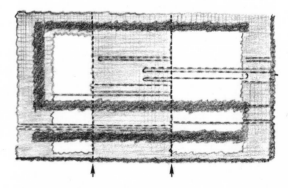

Jacket made of small squares

Three- or four-inch squares of plain weaving in wool can be joined to make a handsome and warm jacket. If you use wool with a loopy, nubbed, or uneven hand-spun texture, it will be even more attractive. Edges and neckline look complete when crocheted, bound with braid, or worked with rows of embroidery stitches.

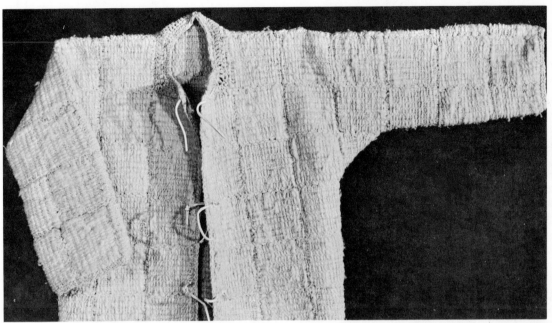

FIGURE 7-5. Jacket fashioned from squares of white handspun wool and pale blue crochet thread. Edges and neckline crocheted. Knotted thongs for ties. Woven on 4-inch loom. (Courtesy of Audio-Visual Services, University of Washington. Florence F. Smith, weaver.)

Project for small weavings

You can bind or make attractive slip-covers for craft notebooks, craft books, or craft magazines, and for other books and periodicals as well. The author, daughter of a bookbinder, used handwoven cotton to hand bind volumes of *Handweaver & Craftsman* magazine.

FIGURE 7-6. Volumes of *Handweaver & Craftsman* magazine hand bound by the author. (Photograph by Hans L. Jorgensen.)

WEAVING STRIPS

Kente Cloth from Ghana

Brilliant colors, very fine silk and cotton, alternating bands of distinctive designs and plain color, woven into long, four-inch wide strips, distinguish Kente cloth. The Kente is woven on the intricate-looking looms pictured in Chapter 2.

Designs

Each design has its own regional significance and symbolic meaning of pattern and color. The pattern may represent a man's social status and family. Its significance for family identification can be compared to that of the clan tartans used in Scotland. Some pattern bands are composed of tapestry-weave geometric forms, others are composed of stripes. Some strips combine both kinds of pattern bands alternating with bands of plain weave in solid color.

Design changes

In recent years, interest from the tourist trade has caused the weavers to make place mats, stoles, bedspreads, and belts from Kente cloth strips. The designs used in these pieces are not true Kente, however, as the people of Ghana prefer not to use their traditional designs for this purpose.

The United Nations Kente Cloth

Ten weavers worked more than three months to weave a 20-foot Kente cloth for the United Nations. The highly appropriate meaning of the design is "One head cannot go into council." (The American version: "Two heads are better than one!")

The colors are vivid: vibrating blue, maroon, gold, green, black, and white.

FIGURE 7-7, 8. Kente cloth stole. Five long strips sewn together. A photograph of this long piece, fringed at each end, is reproduced in two parts. Black warp and plain areas. Colors: white, ochre, yellow, maroon, bright purple-blue. (Courtesy of Mrs. Ruth F. Williams. Photograph by *The Seattle Times.*)

FIGURE 7-9. Single strips of Kente cloth as they come from the loom. (Courtesy of Mrs. Ruth F. Williams. Photograph by *The Seattle Times*.)

From woven strips to sweater

Figures 7-10 and 7-11 show a slipover sweater fabricated from strips of weaving, front and back, with knitted sides and sleeves. The strips were woven on an inkle loom, but could be done on a backstrap, Hungarian, or frame loom. This is an excellent example of total design.

How it was put together

The strips are identical, front and back. Each outside strip is long enough to go up the front and down the back, with no seam on the shoulder. The two inside strips are set down far enough to make a neckline that will slip over the head. The warp on each strip is left for a fringed edge around the neck and bottom. After the knitting was finished, matching fringe was put in with a needle around the rest of the bottom edge.

FIGURE 7-10 Elida Swedine models her distinctive and thoughtfully designed sweater. Black and white wool worsted strips sewn together, sleeves and sides knitted. (Courtesy of Elida Swedine.)

FIGURE 7-11. Woven and knitted sweater. Do you find the one different design unit playfully woven in one strip? (Courtesy of Elida Swedine.)

Bolivian over-the-shoulder bag

Strips of gaily patterned wool, in red, green, and white, are hand-stitched together for an over-the-shoulder carryall bag. A long strip runs up one side and down the other, with enough length for a shoulder strap. Braids and tassels are added for extra adornment. Many of the ideas here can be adapted to weaving strips for a tote or handbag, on a frame or backstrap loom.

Other uses for woven strips

Strips of weaving do not have to be joined together. Narrow strips are useful as belts or ties. Strips can be used like a braid or binding, for trimming jackets and coats, or as borders and edges on draperies, tablecloths, and sweaters. Use them for gay hatbands. Plan a group to be combined into a wall hanging. Use your imagination, and try out all kinds of yarn combinations, stripes, and colors. The photographs of finger-woven bands and those made on Hungarian and frame looms will give you a start on some ideas.

HOW TO ASSEMBLE A HANDWOVEN COLLAGE

A diligent weaver, especially while learning the craft, will weave samples — and more samples. This is the only way to find out for yourself exactly what your loom can do, what happens to color and texture with different weights and spins of yarn. The by-product of all this sampling is a mountain of bits and pieces of weaving — all interesting and helpful, and created by you. You cannot just throw them out; you want to keep them for study but your storage shelves are too full with all the yarns you are collecting. What can you do about it? You can make a wall-hanging collage. This can be a purely decorative wall ornament that, at the same time, serves the purpose of a reference. The appeal of planning, sorting, assembling, laying out the design, and finally sewing it together and enhancing the whole piece with some needlework is strongly reminiscent of family patchwork quilts. You will recognize the same feelings you had when poring over an old pieced quilt that told the story of a fam-

FIGURE 7-12, 13. Girls and animals fore, stripes and patterns aft, on this gay wool bag from Bolivia. (Courtesy of Dr. and Mrs. Palmer Beasley.)

ily's wardrobe. My collage, shown in Figure 7-1, not only shows me what happens to textures and colors, it reminds me of the sampling I have done to achieve just the right shade of blue-green for a friend's necktie, how the loopy border was made for a friend's skirt pocket, a swatch trying out a new rug technique — and there's that sample for the tweed suit!

One approach

First, sort out items by color. You will probably end up with a stack of blue, blue-green, yellow-green, and green; red, orange, and yellow; different shades of white; grays and neutrals. Next, decide which pieces to use in your composition. Sort them out and put away all of the others, for the present. Spread your chosen pieces out so you can see the shapes. Sometimes the shape of a scrap will set the trend of the whole design. Then move them about like a jig-saw puzzle. Overlap, fold, cut, double. Select a background material to blend, contrast, or whatever is best for your design. Pin, sew, embellish, or sew on with embroidery stitches.

Now you have created a double-duty wall decoration for study and for pleasure. And a welcome by-product is more space on your storage shelves.

FOR BEGINNING WEAVERS

For beginners who have no stockpile of swatches, I suggest planning a collage to be made with your learning samples. Keep this use for them in mind and weave for an assembled design. Choose harmonious colors when you are weaving color studies, different techniques, and textures. In this way you will have an elegant weaver's guide as well as a wall decoration when you finish.

SCRAP WEAVING

During several years of house remodeling our family adopted this quotation credited to Martha Washington:
> "We do what we can
> With what we have
> Where we are."

Apply this to weaving and you may come up with some unexpectedly good scrap weaving. For example:

A variety of articles can be made out of thrums. Thrums are a by-product of weaving. They are the ends of warp that are tied to the warp and cloth beams of a loom. When a piece is woven and cut from the loom these short, odd lengths of yarn are left. The busy-ness of a weaver is judged by her thrums boxes. These bits are ideal for an Oriental rug-knot rug (Chapter 8), a woven pile rug, narrow band weaving, or small areas of color in tapestries. You will think of more.

Rags have been weft for weavers since pioneer days when every scrap of cloth was precious and had to be used up to the last thread. The woven round rag rug shown in Chapter 2 is a little different from what we usually think of as a "rag rug."

So many things can be done with cloth strips — with a little imagination and a free-thinking design. Forget, just for now, the typical hit-and-miss woven rag runners and think of the strips of cloth as just so much weft yarn. Colors can be sorted into groups of color families. Widths of strips can vary from about one-half inch, for a finely woven non-fraying cotton or wool, up to a big thick folded strip.

Your warp color and weight will play an important role in your designing. Strips can be dyed, if just the right color is missing. A needed color or texture can be put in by looping or knotting with ends of yarn.

Nylon hose, in an endless range of warm skin tones, are a challenge to a weaver. Cut into fine strips and knotted together, they weave into a beautiful, durable fabric. You can weave a coarse mat or rug from the whole stocking, with or without the feet and tops. Design around the texture of the knots where strips are joined together. You can plan a design of organized knots! Smooth surfaces will result when the strips are folded and overlapped where a new strip is put in.

More weaving with wefts that are not yarn

Scrap weaving leads into thinking about

FIGURE 7-14. Strips of brown mouton and gray caracul fur, on a linen warp, with wool filler, to make a rug of varied texture. (Courtesy of Audio-Visual Services, University of Washington. Hope Munn, weaver.)

other wefts that are not yarn. A stroll through a salvage store will show you that many a fur coat is discarded as too worn to wear, but there is still plenty of beauty there. Cut into strips and woven into a rug, the discarded coat will make a handsome floor covering with years of wear in it (7-14).

An excellent leather fabric can be made from scraps picked out of a glove manufacturer's waste bin. Strips of leather woven on a linen warp make a durable fabric for a tote bag, envelope-style purse, pillows, or upholstery. Leather-strip fabric combined with woven wool or knitted wool will make a good-looking jacket. The leather will make the fabric quite firm; it could be used for the two front sections and the back, with sleeves and sides of wool.

Figure 7-15 shows a piece of fabric woven from such glove-leather strips. These strips are all deer hide in warm shades of creamy white through beige, golden orange, and light brown. The warp is copper colored linen. Originally planned for a jacket, the fabric proved to be a bit too heavy, so this piece was made into pillows. Even very tiny scraps of leather can be cut around into strips and used for weft. Where the strips overlap or are slightly bumpy from uneven cutting, a pleasant casualness is added to the texture.

Many concerns that fabricate articles out of leather have exciting scrap boxes: ask at binderies, diploma binderies, glove makers.

Burlap bag companies, drapery makers, and blanket companies sometimes have scraps from cut-off selvages. These make ideal wefts.

You take it from here — you will probably find some even more beautiful scraps.

FIGURE 7-15. Glove leather strips on a linen warp. Woven by the author.

FIGURE 7-16. Strips of burlap in three colors, coarse and fine yarns. (Courtesy of the Sammamish High School Art Class. Photograph by Clydene Phelps.)

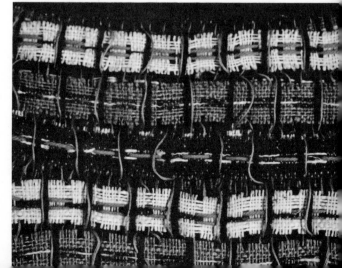

LOOPS

Loops are fast and simple to do and will add interest, pattern, and texture to an otherwise plain fabric. Loops can be high, low, in rows, spots, geometric designs, or fill the whole space. Loops can be in contrasting colors or in a different kind and weight of yarn than the body of the weaving, or both.

The first four rows in the sampler shown in Figure 7-17 are woven with candlewick cotton. This is a many-stranded cotton yarn used in making tufted bedspreads and, of all things, wicks for candles.

How to make loops

Loops are made by lifting a weft yarn up between two warp threads, at intervals across a row. Because they are not knotted to a warp, if they are not held in place by firm beating of the rows before and after, it is easy to pull them out. They are most successful when made on a rather closely set warp, with a row of plain weave on each side of the loop row. Therefore, always work a row of loops against a row of plain weave, and always pick up the loops going in the direction of the weft end, so you will have enough slack.

Plan on using weft yarn about three times the length of the row — more or less, depending upon the size of your yarn and how many loops you pick up.

How to weave with loops

Weave a row of weft, over and under; do not beat down. Between warp threads 1 and 3, insert a knitting needle, picking up a loop of weft (7-18). With a crochet hook, fingers, or tip of a needle, pick up the next loop between warp threads 5 and 7, 9 and 11, and so on, carrying the knitting needle on top of the warp. Pull each loop up the same amount.

The size of the needle you use will help regulate the size of the loop, so use the one that is most suitable for your yarn and design.

Be sure all of the loops twist in the same direction. For clarity, the diagram shows the loops spaced far apart. The sampler shows them close together, with one loop

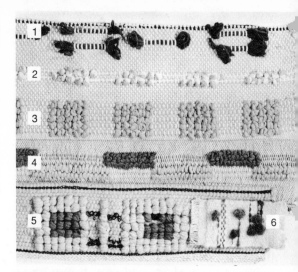

FIGURE 7-17. Loops. You will note that the weft is carried straight across, and where the loops are in isolated spots, the loop color makes a band or stripe. 1, Line and loops. 2, Light and medium orange, woven in together; variegated loops with one row of tabby between. 3, Five rows of loops, one row of tabby between. Five loops wide, to make squares. Doubled candlewick for the loops, single for the tabby. 4, Alternating rectangles of loops, rust, and medium orange, varied widths for interesting spacing. 5, Large cotton rug roving, pale gray and rust, with fine loops of black. 6, Small sample for rug, linen warp, handspun white wool, tufts of unspun natural dark gray wool. All woven by the author.

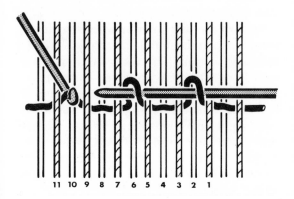

FIGURE 7-18. Method of making loops.

picked up between 1 and 3, 3 and 5, and so on. Remember that you should always weave one or two rows of plain weave after each loop row and beat down firmly to lock the loops in place.

How to make line-and-loops

Line-and-loops or flecks, add a great deal of direction and depth to a plain weave (7-17, 1). Wind a short length of yarn around your fingers several times, flatten this small coil of yarn, place it in the open shed under enough warp threads to hold it in place. Let each end of the loops stick out. When they are all placed in this row, close the shed and weave over and under, beat, and continue with plain weaving. Insert lines-and-loops wherever desired, and any length. If your loom has no heddles, you can weave these in by putting the lines in over and under wherever you want them. Always beat them in firmly, and follow with a row of plain weaving.

TWINING TECHNIQUE

Twining was known and used in basket making as early as 2500 B. C. by many peoples in different parts of the world. It is a simple, finger-controlled weave, employing two wefts, twisted around the warp (7-20). The weaving starts at the top, when woven on a vertical bag loom.

Twining across the warp at the top and bottom of a frame loom is one way to space the warp threads, flattening and firming the warp.

Uses

Twining technique is commonly used in basket weaving. It is used by American Indians of many tribes to weave carrying baskets made of cornhusks or other materials. The twining method is also used by the Chilkat Indians in their blanket weaving.

FIGURE 7-19. A dance shirt of wool, woven in the same technique as the Chilkat blankets. Belongs to members of the Killer Whale clan of the Dukla-Wady tribe, Alaska. (Photograph by William L. Paul, Jr.)

FIGURE 7-20. Method of twining.

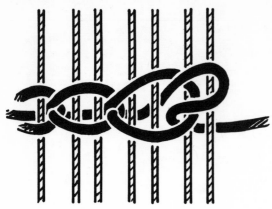

FIGURE 7-21. Chaining.

CHAINING

Chaining, included in the twined weaves, is a very useful technique to know. On a frame or backstrap loom, with a continuous warp, chaining is a quick and satisfactory way to run a line of binding thread close to the end beams. This will space and stabilize the warp and help to even the tension.

Chaining is also very decorative. The loops lie on the surface of the warp, creating a nice texture and pattern. This technique can be used in rugs and wall hangings for borders or spots of loopy surface. If used in rows, it is a good idea to weave one or more spots of plain weave between the rows of chaining.

How to make a row of chaining

Work from left to right. The length of your chaining weft should be several times the width of your warp. Tie a loop at the end of the weft yarn. Place yarn under the whole warp with the end loop at the left, at the edge of the warp. The weft yarn will be picked up from under the warp and brought up in loops between pairs of warps (7-21). With your fingers or a crochet hook, pull the weft up through the first loop between the first pair of warps. This loop lies on top of two warps. Reach down and pull the weft up through this second loop between pairs of warps, and so on across.

If you want to do a single row of chaining, cut the weft end, leaving at least an inch, then pull the cut end through the loop and tighten. Turn the end in around several warp threads to secure. If you wish to weave several rows of chaining, you can use a continuous weft. In this case, do not cut the weft at the end of the row; instead, return it from right to left, over and under. Repeat the procedure of placing the weft under the warps over to the right side and make the second row of chaining. If you wish to make spots or areas of chaining, cut the weft and secure the end as at the end of a row.

In a wall hanging, where you might want a bold and loopy effect, huge chains can be made with heavy yarn or many strands of yarn chained over small groups of warps. See the wall hangings reproduced in color (C-6, C-10).

8 Nine Simple Projects

This chapter gives you how-to-do-it instructions for nine different projects on nine different kinds of simple looms. Before you start on these projects, however, you should read carefully the information about cardboard looms given below.

GENERAL NOTES ON CARDBOARD LOOMS

Use poster board, bristol board, cardboard from the back of tablets, or light cardboard boxes. Gently bend the cardboard to see which direction is the most rigid.

There are many ways to space and hold the warp threads. Four are shown in Figures 2-1, 2, 3, 4 — slits, notches, holes, pins.

By shaping the cardboard loom, it is possible to weave a triangular scarf, a baby bib, a round mat, or coasters on a cardboard circle. All the edges are finished, or selvages, on these. No further edge finish is necessary, unless you wish to put on a decorative border or binding. See Figure 8-21.

Round mats or coasters can be made reversible and very firm by weaving on both sides of the loom. The loom itself then becomes the inside layer between the two woven sides (8-15).

A cardboard loom limits you somewhat in size, but many things — coverlets, boxy jackets, baby blankets, rugs — can be woven in small units and sewed together as explained and illustrated in Chapter 7; two ways to sew pieces together are shown in Chapter 6, Figure 6-19 A, B.

The size of your loom will depend upon the size you want your finished weaving. If your weaving must be an exact size, be sure to make all of the allowances given below. (These measurements are approximate. They depend upon the kind of yarn you are using, and what you are weaving.)

Allow $1/4$ inch at the top and $1/4$ inch at the bottom, for space you will not be able to weave.

Allow $1/2$ inch to 1 inch for seams or hems. Add to top, bottom, or side measurements — do not forget the sides if you are to sew pieces together. If the seams will overlap, an allowance is necessary. If they will just come together, no extra width is needed.

Make sure you include all allowances for the correct size of your finished weaving. Make sure your loom is the correct size.

The weaving takes up some of the width and length of the warp, especially if a coarse yarn is used. The piece will be a little smaller when it is taken from the loom and the tension of the warp is released. Allow another 1/4 inch to 1/2 inch for this, especially if your weaving must be an exact size.

Allow for shrinkage in washing. If you are in doubt about size after shrinkage, wash the first unit before you continue a project of many small units, to see what the shrinkage will be. Cotton carpet warp will shrink some. Wools can be blocked to size and, if carefully handled, most of them will not shrink much.

Important: When you measure and mark across the ends for the spacing of the warp, be sure that each mark is directly opposite each mark on the other end so your warp will be straight and parallel to the sides of the loom.

THE PROJECTS: STEP-BY-STEP INSTRUCTIONS

To help you learn how to do some of the weaving techniques we bring you, and how best to use some of the different kinds of simple looms, we have worked out a number of projects to give you a start. Do not feel that you should follow them exactly, as far as yarns, colors, and designs are concerned, but I do suggest that you follow the techniques. When you have learned the techniques, you can go on from there with adaptions and combinations to your heart's content.

Family Projects

Some of these projects will work out best if several members of the family participate. Because small hands may not be able to cut the slits or notches in stiff cardboard, this step will be a good job for an older brother or sister. It will help teach measuring and cutting. Or perhaps here grandmother or grandfather can be of assistance. Father, grandfather, or big brother can help by cutting board loom parts, making a frame and reinforcing the corners, cutting slits or notches or holes in tough material, pounding the big nails. Mother and grandmother can help select yarns, give a hand in the warping and in preparing wefts for weaving, and do the sewing and finishing. Everyone can plan designs and help decide what to weave. It might be enjoyable for everyone to work on parts of a rug or coverlet — turning the project into a sociable old-fashioned weaving bee, like the quilting parties in earlier days.

FIGURE 8-1. Doll-house rug. Plain weave, Ghiordes knot loops. Woven by the author.

HOW TO WEAVE A DOLL-HOUSE RUG
ON A FLAT CARDBOARD LOOM

At this point, please read once again the general notes on cardboard looms at the beginning of this chapter.

The directions given below are for the little rug shown here. This one is about 3 inches by 5½ inches, finished size. If you want a larger one, make your cardboard loom about one-half inch larger, *in each dimension,* than the finished size you prefer.

You will need

> One piece of poster board, 3½ inches by 7 inches.
> Cotton carpet warp or string, about 2½ yards.
> Weft: knitting worsted, about 23 yards white, 3 yards dark.
> Blunt-end tapestry needle.
> Pencil, wooden skewer, knitting needle, or small dowel, to use for gauge to make loops of uniform size.
> Fork, for a beater.
> Scissors, pencil, ruler.

How to make the cardboard loom

Measure ¼ inch in from the short end of your cardboard. Draw a line across, all the way. Repeat at the other end. Measure in from the edge ¼ inch on the line. Mark. Continue marking each ¼ inch all the way across, 13 times. Cut slits at each mark, down to the line. Repeat at the other end, making sure that the slits are exactly opposite, so the warp will be straight (8-2).

Now you are ready to warp

Tie a double knot in the end of your carpet warp. Slip this into the first slit at the left side, a, at the top end of the loom. The knot should be at the back. Hold the loom in your left hand while bringing the warp yarn down through the first bottom slit, 1, then over to the right and up through slit 2; bring it up to the top and through slit b, over to the right and up through slit, c, and so on, until you reach the last slit at the right (8-3). Bring the warp around the end, and tie it at the back. Pull the warp so it is just taut, but not taut enough to bow the

cardboard. As you bring the warp to the right between the slits, press and push down to the bottom of the slit with your left finger. Stretch each warp thread about the same amount, so the tension will be as even as possible.

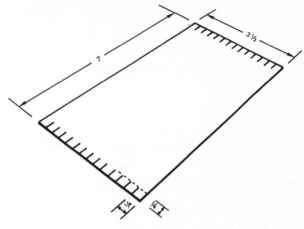

FIGURE 8-2. Flat cardboard loom.

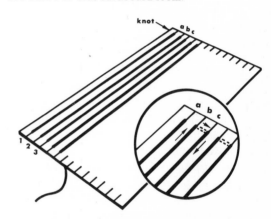

FIGURE 8-3. Flat cardboard loom. How to warp.

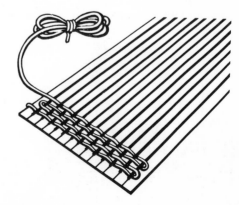

FIGURE 8-4. Plain weave on flat cardboard loom.

121

Now you are ready to weave
Techniques: Plain weave, Ghiordes knot loops

Make a butterfly or bobbin with your weft yarn (Figures 6-17, 6-18) or thread the blunt-end needle with about 18 inches of the white wool weft yarn. Weave over and under the warp, back and forth, four times, as shown in Figure 8-4. Tuck the end of the weft in, by turning it in around the outside warp, weaving it in over three warps between the first and second rows. Put in one row of loops.

How to make the Ghiordes knot loops

Make a butterfly of weft yarn. Start at the left side of your loom and bring the weft up between the first and second warp threads. Leave an end of the weft yarn about an inch long to be woven in later, after the knot row is completed, as you did at the beginning end. Place your gauge (I used a wooden skewer from the butcher shop) on the top of the warp, just above the last row of plain weave.

Take the bobbin up over the gauge, under the left warp, over, around, and under the right warp, down under the gauge pulling down to tighten around the two warps. Then back up and under the next warp (on left), beginning the next knot. The loop should not be pulled tight against the gauge; pull just enough to make the loop the size you want, uniform with the rest of the loops. The yarn that goes around the gauge is your loop on the surface of the fabric; the yarn around the two warp threads is the knot holding the loop firmly in place. Follow the path of the weft in the drawing, and you will be able to see just where it goes (8-5).

When the row of knots is complete, leave the gauge in place while you weave over and under from right to left. Turn the beginning weft end in now. Beat in with the fork, firmly against the gauge. Weave another row from left to right, beat in, then carefully pull the gauge out. Beat again, pressing the two rows of plain weave into the row of knots.

Although the directions call for the same bobbin of weft to be used for the loop rows and the rows in between, if you want to use a different color or different kind of yarn for the background the weft can be cut after the last loop is made. Loops can be started and stopped wherever you wish, in rows or groups. Just be sure to weave in the inch left at cut ends.

Continue in this way: two rows of plain weave, one row of loops, four rows of plain weave; two rows of dark gray plain weave, one row white, two rows gray, six rows white — all plain weave. And so on, weaving rows of plain and rows of loops as you wish. After the last row of loops at the other end I did four rows of plain weave, cut the weft, and tucked the end back in as we did at the beginning.

Pack the last few rows in as much as you can. Then, when the weaving is removed from the loom, it will completely fill all of the warp.

How to remove the rug from the loom

Gently push each loop of warp off the cardboard, bending the cardboard slightly if necessary. Now you have a finished small rug like the one shown in Figure 8-1. If you have been careful not to pull the edge too much, it will be nice and flat. If necessary, you may steam press it lightly on the back, without pressure.

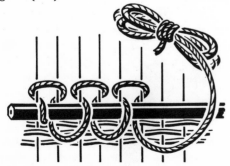

FIGURE 8-5. Method of making Ghiordes knot.

FIGURE 8-6. Ghiordes knots, cut and uncut. Handspun wool on linen. Woven by the author.

HOW TO WEAVE TAPESTRY ON A CRESCENT CARDBOARD LOOM

Before you begin your tapestry on the Crescent loom, please be sure to read the chapter on Tapestry carefully. There you will find complete directions on how to prepare your design cartoon, how to interlock the wefts where there are color changes, how to outline a design, along with many helpful hints and suggestions on tapestry weaving, which, I believe, will answer any questions that come up. I hope you will have made a tapestry-technique sampler, before attempting a complete tapestry. Also, refer back to the general notes on cardboard looms given earlier.

You will need

One piece of firm but flexible cardboard, such as poster board, $5^{1}/_{2}$ inches by 7 inches.

Scotch tape, 1 inch wide.

Common pins.

Warp thread: cotton carpet warp.

Weft: wool yarn, knitting worsted.

Fork for beater.

Blunt-end needles: one for each color and a few extra, depending on color changes you have — and how often you want to thread and unthread needles!

Ruler, pencil, scissors.

Design cartoon on squared paper.

Colored pencils, if you choose to color your design.

FIGURE 8-8. Plain weave tapestry technique, outlining. Design derived from Peruvian weaving. Woven by the author.

How to make the loom

This loom is curved into a crescent shape by the tension put on the warp threads. At a $5^{1}/_{2}$-inch end of the cardboard, measure in $^{1}/_{4}$ inch and mark each $^{1}/_{4}$ inch all the way across to within $^{1}/_{4}$ inch of the other side. Repeat at the other end, making sure that the marks are exactly opposite so your warp will be straight. Put scotch tape across each end of the cardboard, so that half of the tape is on the top side of the cardboard and half on the back, covering the edge like a binding. The pins to hold the warp are pushed into the edge of the cardboard, one at each mark. The tape reinforces the edge and helps to hold the pins in. Push the pins in carefully, about $^{1}/_{2}$ inch, so that the points do not come through. Put tape and pins along the other end of the cardboard in the same way.

Prepare your design

Your design on squared paper may be taped to the loom before the warp is put on, or, if the design is simple, you may just keep it beside you for reference.

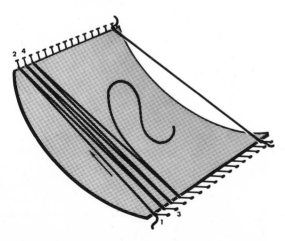

FIGURE 8-7. Crescent cardboard loom.

FIGURE 8-9. Design Cartoon on squared paper.

Draw your design on squared paper having eight squares to the inch (8-9). Your loom will be warped 16 threads to the inch, but for this project weaving is done over two warps at once, therefore the weaving will be eight to the inch. Each square equals the pair of warp threads over which you are weaving. Outline each area with heavy pencil or pen lines so you will easily see when it is time to change color. You may want to color the different design areas. For a small and simple design such as this, you may want to do as I did and just indicate in pencil the different shades and outlines for the few colors.

If you followed our advice and tried out the tapestry techniques on a sampler, you will know what you can and what you cannot do; this should help you in your choice of design.

For your beginning tapestry, use a simple, linear design that will require several changes of color. It is best not to put in any fine detail for this starter. Use slanting, straight, and curved lines. Slanting and curving lines do not require the yarn to be interlocked where the color is changed. A design adapted from an ancient Peruvian motif of two fish was chosen for the tapestry shown in Figure 8-8. (See Chapter 2 for more on Peruvian designs.) The design seemed appropriate to the technique be-

cause much Peruvian weaving was done in this plain-weave interlocked tapestry with limning (outlining) of the design. Knitting worsted and a wool yarn slightly heavier than worsted was used for weft, on a cotton carpet warp.

The finished tapestry is 5½ inches by 7 inches, which is the size of the loom used. The sides of the tapestry curve out somewhat because the yarn was not pulled quite tightly enough. The weft should be sufficiently relaxed to completely cover the warp — not so taut that it draws in at the sides, but just right to keep the edges straight. This procedure is quite tricky to do and you must be constantly aware of what is happening to the width of your work. Do try to draw a design of your own, but for this project, use an idea with the same problems of joining colors, outlining, and including a border, as in the example here.

Now you are ready to warp the loom

This is a continuous warp, so you will use the thread directly from the spool. At this point refer again to Figure 8-7. To help make the cardboard a smooth crescent shape, tie one length of warp from the top pin to the bottom pin on the right end of the loom. Then begin the warping at the left end. Knot one end of the warp around the first pin, 1; take the warp thread up to the first pin at the top, 2; around it and down to 3. Around pin 3, back up to pin 4, and so on until the warp has been taken around each pin in succession.

After two or three warp lengths are on, as you wind the warp gently pull it enough to slightly round or bow the cardboard. This will create a space under the warp, making it easier to weave. Check the single warp tied at the other end, to be sure the loom is equally bowed. There should be about a ¾-inch space at the center, between the cardboard and the warp. Tie the end of the warp around the last pin. Even out the tension on each line of warp. Remove the temporary single warp and wind on the last warp thread. Tie this to the last pin.

Now you are ready to weave

Remember to weave over pairs of warp threads. Where a warp is mentioned in the directions, it means the pair, used as one. This is such a small warp that it will be easiest to use a blunt-end tapestry needle instead of a shuttle or butterfly. Also, in this case, it is not too tedious to weave over and under in both directions without a shed. On such a miniature weaving, a shed stick would be useful for only a few inches and then it would just be in the way.

Thread your needle with the border color, weave several rows over and under, beating them firmly in as close to the pins as you can.

Weave as many rows as necessary for your border width. Begin the side borders. Right to left, weave over three warps and interlock with background color (8-10).

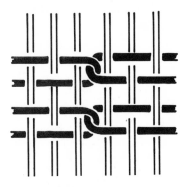

FIGURE 8-10. Tapestry techniques. Interlock.

Weave a row of background all the way across to third warp from the left. Interlock with the border color. Complete the row by weaving the left border. Next row: left to right, weave the border, interlock with the background, weave the background up to the beginning of the center design.

The outlining yarn will be carried up as the design is woven, like an overcast stitch over the warp, serving as the link between the center design and the background (8-11).

On this tapestry, after the center design and outlining were started, seven needles were used, two each for the border, the background, and the outlining yarns on both sides of the center, and one needle

FIGURE 8-11. Tapestry techniques. Limning or outlining a design area.

for the central design. An eighth needle was added when the light part of the central design was reached. This does sound a little confusing, but if you study the drawing (8-11), which shows how the outlining thread relates to the weaving on each side of it, and do some sampling, I think you will get the idea. More on how to do outlining is given in the Sampler section, Chapter 3.

Complete your tapestry by weaving several rows for the top border, pushing the weft down and crowding the rows in a bit too closely so that when the piece is taken from the loom the weft can be moved up a little to cover the warp. Weave the end of the weft in, then cut. You have now woven a tapestry.

How to remove from the loom

You can either lift the weaving off the pins by cupping the flexible cardboard slightly to relax the tension, or you can remove the pins from the ends of the loom. If you wish you can sew a row of chain stitching across each end in the border or background color, as I did, to cover any warps that show through at the end and to give a nice finish. If necessary, you may press or block your tapestry. Refer to the Tapestry section for instructions on how to do this.

FIGURE 8-12. A red sun with lacy rays of vivid oranges, fuchsias, and pinks was woven on a home-made plywood circle loom. The solid center was woven round and round, then the warps were separated and woven into segments. Wool warp was used to withstand the stress of distortion. The weft is handspun wool. It is appropriately mounted on weathered board. (Courtesy of *Handweaver & Craftsman*, New York. Mary Ellen Cranston-Bennett, weaver. Purchased by the City of San Francisco.)

WEAVING IN CIRCLES

Here is a choice of three ways to prepare the edge of a cardboard circle loom (8-13 and 2-8):

A. Slits cut around the edge.
B. Notched edge.
C. Pins stuck into the thickness of the cardboard — this type requires a thick, quite stiff cardboard.

Our working drawing shows a loom with slits.

How to weave a small mat or coaster on a cardboard circle

You will need

One circle, cut out of cardboard. About 3 inches in diameter for a coaster, about 5 inches in diameter for a hot-dish mat.
Warp: Jute or cotton carpet warp.
Weft: Jute or cotton rug yarn.
Large blunt-end tapestry needle.
Pencil, ruler, scissors.

How to make and warp the loom

Divide the edge of the circle into an odd number of equal spaces and cut in a slit about ³⁄₈ of an inch long at each mark. For a 3-inch coaster cut 15 slits. Tie a knot in the end of the warp thread and slip it through one of the slits so that the knot is on the back, out of your way. Study the working drawing in Figure 8-13 and note that the warp is carried from 1 across to 8, under to the left, up at 9. From 9 it goes across to 2, then under to the right, up at 3, and so on around. The last slit is 15, and here the warp is brought up through, carried under all of the warp threads where they cross at the center, and brought out between 7 and 8.

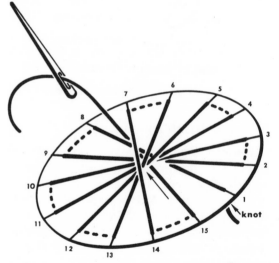

FIGURE 8-13. Flat circle cardboard loom. How to warp.

To draw all of the warp together and form a good center, make a chain stitch as follows: bring the thread around in a loop on top of all warp threads, holding the thread down with your left thumb, taking it down under all threads between 6 and 7, out between 13 and 14, on top of the loop (8-14). Pull together, and you have a chain stitch binding all of the warps together, and a good beginning to weave around.

Begin the weaving under 14, over 15, and so on. Weave as closely as you can all the way out to the edge. The loops of warp around the edge will make a finished border.

After the mat is slipped off the loom, you can run a coarse or contrasting yarn through the loops for a ridged edge. A blanket stitch can be worked around for another kind of edge. The beginning knot in the warp is untied and the end woven in.

FIGURE 8-15. Two-sided coaster woven on circle cardboard loom (Figure 8-16). Green Jute. Woven by the author.

You will need

One circle, cut out of cardboard. About 5 inches in diameter for a hot-dish mat.
Warp: jute, or cotton carpet warp.
Weft: jute, cotton rug yarn, raffia.
Large blunt-end tapestry needle.
Pencil, ruler, scissors.

How to make the loom

The loom is made just like the one shown for the single mat except for a small hole put in the center. Slits are cut, evenly spaced, all around the edge (8-16).

How to warp the loom

Thread the needle with a long length of warp. Put a knot at the end of the warp. Bring the warp up through a slit. Take it down through the hole in the center, out to the edge, and up through the next slit.

The warp goes round and round, first on one side and then the other. Knot the end of the warp at the last slit. The warp ends will be covered by the weaving.

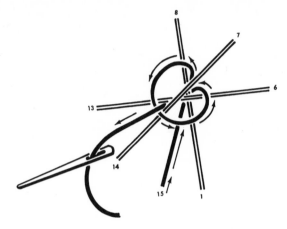

FIGURE 8-14. How to make beginning chain stitch for center of weaving on cardboard circle loom.

Tips to help make the work go easily

When you have to start a new weft, cut the end of jute or coarse yarn on a slant so the ends will feather out and blend into the weaving. Any protruding ends can be clipped off later. When you weave in the new weft yarn, hold the end with your thumb as you pull it through so that it won't be pulled out.

How to make a double mat

A reversible, double-thick mat, pad, or coaster can be made on a flat cardboard circle loom. You weave a kind of sandwich, using the loom itself as the filling with weaving on each side of it. The cardboard stays in the middle, making the mat firm and a sure protection for the table when used under hot dishes. Each side is woven independently. Try a different color on each side, for variety.

FIGURE 8-16. Flat circle cardboard loom with hole in center, to weave two-sided mat. How to warp.

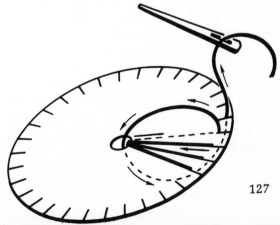

How to weave the mat

Thread your needle with weft yarn. Start weaving over and under at the center, tucking the end under the warp. Weave over and under, as far out to the edge as possible. Cut the weft, then push the cut end in under the weaving. Now turn the loom over and weave the other side in the same way, from the center out to the very edge.

How to finish the edge

There are several ways to finish the edge in order to cover up any bit of the loom that may show. A closely set overcast stitch all around works well. Blanket stitching done all around in one direction, with another row facing it, done in the opposite direction, is a neat border. Several strands of yarn can be couched on, or a cross stitch, catching in each layer and drawing them together, can be used. The example shown was made of jute on both sides, the edge finished with the blanket stitching as described.

HOW TO WEAVE A SMALL RUG ON A WHEEL OR HOOP LOOM

Sometimes a small round rug, a round chair pad, or other round woven item is wanted. For such purposes, the hoop-type looms are ideal, and lots of fun to work on.

The loom

To weave a circle, use a bicycle rim, hula hoop, barrel hoop, or a large embroidery hoop — whatever you can come by to make the size rug you want. The same method will work on a smaller scale, using the usual smaller embroidery hoops for small mats, pads, or round doll-house rugs. The wheel rug photographed was made entirely out of rag strips (8-17). Heavy cotton rug roving would be suitable for the whole rug, or just for the warp, with rag strips for the weft. A pleasing stripe can be planned out from the cloth strips you have; a combination of yarn and cloth would provide interest and variation. Colors can be dyed to fit a color scheme. The directions here are for a small all-rag rug.

FIGURE 8-17. Rag rug on wheel loom. Warp, strips of white sheets, and black cotton. Weft: black, sky blue, blue and white print, light red, and light blue. (Courtesy of Interlake Manor, Bellevue, Washington. Woven by a patient.) Pillow woven over foam pillow form as the loom. Heavy wool in tones of grayed greens, golds, and blues. Woven by the author.

You will need

A hoop.
Rag strips.
Scissors.
Needle and sewing thread.

How to warp the wheel loom

Strips of cloth 1½ to 2 inches wide are folded with the raw edges turned in.

Tie a strip around the rim at 1 and knot it firmly (8-18). Take it across, pulling it taut, and tie at 4. Continue as in Figure 8-18, with two more strips. Then tie a strip, 7, near strip 1. This will be your first weaving strip, or weft. Take this strip to the center where the strips cross. Weave it over 1, under 2, and so on around, for two rows. Then push to center with fingers to make a tight, firm center. Continue weaving around for several more rows. Then add some additional warp strips, as follows:

FIGURE 8-18. Wheel rim loom. How to warp.

FIGURE 8-19. How to add additional warp threads on wheel rim loom.

How to add extra warp strips

Refer to Figures 8-18 and 8-19 for this procedure. Next to 1, tie the end of a strip, take it to the center, to the last row of weft; under, and up over and back to the rim next to 2. Tie to the rim. Repeat this all the way around, between each pair of the first warp strips.

Proceed with the weaving, over and under, around and around, until the warps are again too far apart. Add more warp strips, always taking them under and over the last row of weaving. Continue in this fashion until you have filled all of the space to the edge. Every row is pushed toward the center, so your mat will be firm and even.

If you want an extremely firm or solid result, push the wefts in very close. Tuck the ends of the wefts in as you start new ones, and weave over them for a few inches. The ends will all pack in and not be seen.

How to remove the rug from the loom

With matching or blending sewing thread, sew small running stitches around the edge, so the last row will not ravel out. Untie each warp strip. The ends of the warp will make a fringe all the way around.

How to finish the edge

The warp ends can be trimmed off evenly, or, if you wish a finer fringe, each strip can be cut once or twice, up to within 1/4 inch of the line of sewing. You may like the effect of knotting each two end-strips in a double knot, all the way around. If you wish, a round or two of machine stitching can be put in through the last row of weft.

HOW TO WEAVE A ROUND PILLOW WITH NO LOOM AT ALL

Thinking about all ways to weave in the round, we chanced on the idea of using a polyfoam pillow form as the loom, and of weaving the cover directly on it. This is just a larger, thicker version of weaving on a round cardboard loom. It turned out so well, and was so amusing and fast to do, we had it photographed for you to see (8-17).

How to warp and weave the pillow

Wool yarn was used for both warp and weft, which gives a very rich, soft effect. Warp was put on around and around, across to one side, down across the back, up and over again. Double and triple strands of wool in soft shades of blue-green, gray-green, yellow-green, and gold, were put in over and under the warp.

Push the rows down, very close together, so that the pillow form will not show through; otherwise the yarns will pack and form gaps with use. Some rows are overcast stitch; some chain stitch. The variation in the number of strands of wool and changes of stitch make an interesting texture and pattern. The other side was woven in about the same way, but with a selection of slightly lighter colors. Round pillow covers are a bit difficult to sew from fabric and we think this idea is a great time and trouble-saver.

FIGURE 8-20. This unusual big handsome sunflower was also woven on a plywood circle loom. Golden yellow and brown wools are used on a jute and sisal warp. Wrapped and plain weave. Weathered boards serve as background and frame. (Courtesy of *Handweaver & Craftsman*, New York. Mary Ellen Cranston-Bennett, weaver.)

FIGURE 8-21. Light blue cotton baby bib, woven on board loom to shape. Woven by the author.

HOW TO WEAVE A BABY BIB TO SHAPE ON A BOARD LOOM

A fond grandmother or grandfather might like to weave a collection of bibs for the grand-babies. Perhaps a sister or brother would like to do this for the new baby. Bibs can be woven on a cardboard loom, but if you want to weave several bibs, the board loom is much more practical and will last through any number of weaving projects. See the Idea Page, Chapter 6, for more shaped weaving plans. The bibs come off the loom completely finished — all edges are selvages, and the ties are woven in. The cotton yarns will shrink in washing, therefore allow at least an inch all around, so the bib will be the size you want, after washing.

You will need

> One piece of plywood, $^1/_2$ or $^3/_4$ inch thick.
> Small-headed nails.
> Warp: cotton carpet warp.
> Weft: any soft cotton yarn, rug yarn, or novelty yarn with uneven texture. I used cotton ratine for the main part, with cotton rug yarn for the stripe and ties.
> Tapestry needle.
> Small, flat shuttle.
> Pencil, scissors, paper for pattern.

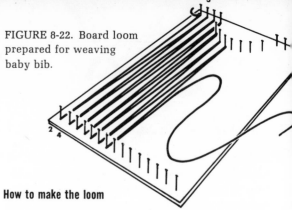

FIGURE 8-22. Board loom prepared for weaving baby bib.

How to make the loom

Cut a paper pattern of your bib and draw around it on the board. Pound nails in, following the shoulder and neck lines, and across the bottom (8-22).

How to warp

Wind the warp on from the spool. Knot the end around nail 1, carry down to nail 2, around it and back up to 3, and so on to the last nail. Knot the warp around the last one and cut.

How to weave

Wind the weft around a small stick shuttle, or prepare a bobbin, or thread the weft into a tapestry needle. Start at the bottom and weave up. Weave over and under, turning the end of the weft in around several warp threads.

Weave in contrasting stripes, a small design in tapestry techniques (see Tapestry, Chapter 3), or just use a contrasting yarn for the ties.

When you reach the curved neckline, weave back and forth, between the nails, following the neckline curve, first on one side, then the other. Each narrow width is woven as a completely separate bit.

When you reach the top at the shoulder, cut and tuck in the end of the weft. Thread your needle with three strands of weft, long enough to braid and still remain long enough to tie comfortably around the baby's neck. These are put into the same shed. Weave them in one at a time, or all three at once. Just to be sure that the long end for the tie comes out at the inside — at the neck. Weave the ties in the same way on each side. Braid, then knot the ends. Carefully lift your piece from the nails. Now you have woven a bib.

ORIENTAL KNOT RUG: TWO-WARP LOOM

Design your rug and know the size of your units before you set up your loom. Make the loom the best length for your finished strips. For example: if your rug will be composed of 24-inch strips sewn together, make your loom with the weaving space about 12 inches long. Allow a little for take-up of the warp in the knotting process — the strip pulls in a bit when removed from the loom. Then you will have to move the warps only once to weave a strip 24 inches long; 12 inches is a comfortable reach, but try it for yourself. Perhaps a child would be happier reaching only 10 inches. A grandmother may be able to reach 15 inches comfortably. This loom is custom-made to fit you and what you are weaving.

How and what

For a very lush, firm rug, with standup pile, pack the knots in just as closely as you can.

Then try some more loosely packed. Try different lengths and weights of yarn, too, and see what depth of pile you like best. This way, you can judge just what density you need for your particular purpose and kind of yarn.

Try using several strands of fine yarn, matching or blending colors, instead of a single yarn in each knot. Try a thick and thin yarn together. These are secrets of the lively color and richness seen in Scandinavian rugs.

Two-inch lengths are about the minimum you could use easily. If you want your finished rug to have a shorter nap, it can be sheared after the units have been sewn together.

If you are using uneven yarn scraps, you can cut them to size before knotting, or use them as they are and even up the surface after the strips are woven or after the rug is put together. You may find you like an uneven, shaggy effect.

Knotting jute over jute or cotton warp will give you a very durable doormat.

Cotton or wool in dark or bright colors, not too tightly packed, makes rough-and-

FIGURE 8-23. Oriental knot loom weaving: Cut wefts, one knotted pile strip, sections of pile strips sewed together for a deep-piled rug. Planned design can be noted. When these units of design are repeated, the overall rug will have a subtle checked and stripe pattern. Woven by the author.

ready floor pillows that will take hard wear.

Design of the rug pictured

For this rug I worked out an all-over design and planned colors to be repeated in certain areas. In the section photographed (8-23) you can see the design taking shape. The single strip shows how the rows of the design are knotted to bring the spots of color at the right place. Four colors and two weights of rug cotton were used: copper, light brown, and dark brown in medium-sized rug yarn; large rug roving in white. Each knot is a combination of two or three of these colors.

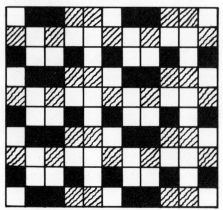

Here is how we put it down on paper, to keep everything straight:

☐ Light brown and white.

▨ Light and dark brown.

■ Dark brown and copper.

Pairs of rug yarn, five knots in each inch. Pairs of one rug yarn, one roving, four knots each inch. Strips were knotted in order, cut, and pinned together ready for sewing. This is a small sample, but the design method is the same as for a full-size rug.

HOW TO WEAVE A RUG ON AN ORIENTAL KNOT LOOM

The two-warp loom, Turkish knot loom, and Oriental knot loom are all the same. Tying knots over just two warp threads is really getting down to fundamentals. The process of building a rug from strips of knots is rewarding, easy, and certainly does not require any elaborate equipment (8-24).

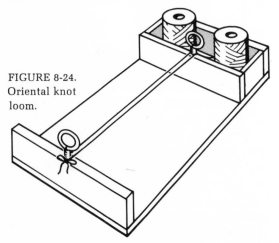

FIGURE 8-24. Oriental knot loom.

You will need

One piece of board, 1 inch thick, (or $3/4$-inch plywood) about 12 inches long and 6 inches wide.

Two 6-inch end pieces of 1- by 2-inch board.

Two screw-eyes.

One thumbtack.

A small box for spools.

Warp: cotton carpet warp, 2 spools.

Weft: cotton rug yarn, wool worsted.

Square of cardboard to measure and and cut lengths of weft.

Scissors.

Squared paper, if you plan a design.

How to make the loom

Nail the two 1- by 2-inch pieces on the 12-inch board — one piece at the end, the other in far enough to allow a platform for the spool box. Measure and mark the center of each end piece. Screw one screw eye into the top of each end piece on the center mark. Push the thumbtack in an inch or two from the screw eye at the spool end. Place the spool box. Now you are ready to put on the warp.

How to warp the knot loom

Put the two spools of warp in the box. Draw the end of warp from each spool toward the opposite screw-eye, taking one on each side, which will space the warp just enough. Wrap the ends around the shank of the screw eye once or twice, tie in a bow knot. At the spool end, wrap the warps around the shank of the eye two or three times, take the two ends around the thumbtack to help hold the tension. The warp threads should be quite tight.

Now you are ready to weave

Prepare your cut strips of weft either of these two ways:

Around a piece of cardboard —

For pile about $1^1/2$ inches deep, cut lengths of yarn about 3 inches long. Wind yarn around cardboard $1^1/2$ by 5 inches. Cut yarn along one edge (8-25A).

Around a block of wood —

Cut a ¼-inch deep groove in a block of wood that is 3 inches around. The groove provides a slot for the scissors when cutting the 3-inch pieces of yarn. Wind yarn the length of the block. If you are making quite a large rug, this is a worthwhile tool to have; it can be made 8 or 10 inches long and a good many strips can be wound and cut at one time (8-25B).

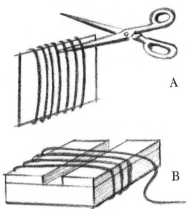

FIGURE 8-25, A and B. Two ways to measure your weft for cutting into even strips for use on the Oriental knot loom.

How to make the knot

Study Figure 8-26. Lay a strip across the warps. Take ends around the warp and up between, keeping the ends even. Pull up, then down. Warp threads will come together. Pull knot down toward you as far as you can. Repeat, pulling each knot up tightly on the two warp threads and down firmly against the previous knots. It is a good idea to do a sample strip of knots first. Every inch or two try a different degree of firmness. Push the knots down very snugly, then for an inch or so not quite so tightly.

FIGURE 8-26. Method of making the Oriental knot, with cut wefts.

When the warp is full, untie the bow-knot — the end toward you — and unfasten the other end. Slip the last knot up the warp a little way so you can put the strip over the screw eye, between two knots. Stretch the warp and fasten as before at the spool end. Tighten up the last knot, and proceed with more knots. Repeat this moving down and retying process until a strip is made to the length you need. Because the warp is used from the spool, an almost endless strip of knots can be made without cutting.

If you want to use short lengths sewn together, side by side, you should weave each strip just that length.

How to fasten warp ends and remove strip from loom

Unfasten the warps at the spool end, cut, leaving several inches of warp. Tie in a double knot, so the rug knots will not slip off or loosen. Untie the other end and knot in the same way. When your rug is put together, all these ends can be threaded back in and clipped off so they will not show.

Helpful hints

If you are making a very long strip to sew round and round like a braided rug, it is a good idea to coil the strips in a box beside you as you weave.

If you have a planned design and want spots of color to be in the proper place when the strips are sewn together, pin each strip in order with a safety pin as you remove it from the loom.

If you are doing quite a large rug, you may want to cut a few dozen pieces of each color, knot them, and then do some more cutting. Alternating the two may provide a welcome change of pace. Later, you can begin to sew some of the strips as you go.

After the first few inches of knotting, you will know about how many pieces are needed per inch and you will be able to estimate the total number to cut.

How to sew the strips together

Work from the knotted side. Use strong carpet thread or the same cotton warp you used on the loom. A blunt-end needle will slip readily through the knots. If you are sewing the strips side by side, pin two strips together at the end and along every few inches for a short space. Knot the thread or sew over and over to start. Sew from strip to strip in a zigzag stitch through every second or third knot, pulling the stitches up so the strips just meet.

Try to line up the knots side by side. This is especially important if you have a planned design and want areas of color to be lined up. If you did not pin the strips when you removed them from the loom, as I suggested before, the matched spots should be pinned together now, then the knots in between eased in as you sew. The finished result, on the back, will look just as though the rug had been woven on a wide warp, all at once.

For an oval, square, or round rug, the strips are sewn together in the same way as the straight strips. The short length of warp at the end of the knotted strips can be tied together to make an endless strip — the joining will be hidden in the depths of the pile. As you join lengths together, tie warps in a double knot, then weave the ends into the knots for half an inch or so. No edge fringe or hem is necessary on these rugs.

Finishing

If you expect your rug to get heavy wear, especially on a hard floor, you can sew a strip of twill tape across the ends to further secure the edge.

To keep the rug from slipping on a waxed floor, you can paint the back of it with liquid latex rug backing available in most housewares, department, and hardware stores.

HOW TO WEAVE A SWEDISH KNOT TAPESTRY

Important: Before starting a Swedish knot project, please re-read the following four sections:

Looms. To help you decide which kind of loom you prefer to use. For a Swedish knot tapestry, we suggest the canvas-stretcher frame or another kind of frame loom.

General tapestry notes. Many questions will arise on how to proceed, and we think most of the answers are there.

Design. How to make the design cartoon or ink the design on the warp.

Warping. How to warp a frame loom.

You will need

A frame loom. Choose a frame with inside dimensions about 3 or 4 inches wider and 2 or 3 inches longer than the finished width of your tapestry. This will give you plenty of working room inside of the frame and allow for a heading at the top and bottom.

Warp thread: cotton carpet warp, or linen.

Weft yarn: wool worsted, wool rug yarn, or needlepoint yarn.

Blunt-end tapestry needles and/or prepared bobbins.

Design cartoon, or design inked on the warp. Check to be sure that your design is facing the right way, especially where there are numbers or letters. Remember, you are weaving from the back of the tapestry.

How to weave

Because the working side is the reverse of the finished piece, all yarn-ends will be on this side. Traditionally, these ends are not darned in, so it is correct for the back to be shaggy with cut ends. Turn the frame over every so often to check and see that all of the warp is covered. If there is an empty space, knots can be filled in. The right side will appear the same, regardless of which direction you weave.

FIGURES 8-27, 28. Front and back of Swedish knot tapestry. Note the ties at sides to keep the edges straight. Design inspired by what weaver saw from her window, high above Puget Sound. (Courtesy of Sonia Ann Beasley, weaver.)

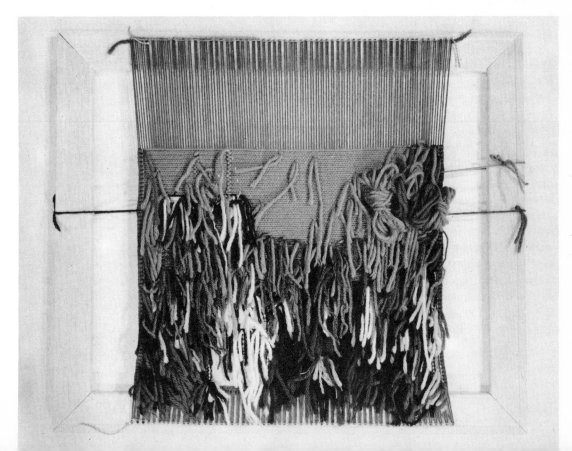

You may work each row always from the right, or each row always from the left, or back and forth, right to left and left to right. Work in whichever direction you find is best for you. Look at the drawings showing how the knot is worked when you change direction (8-30, 31). Your work will be smoother if, in any one row, you weave in just one direction.

Some parts of the design can be built up independently if the curve does not overhang part of the warp that is not yet covered. We have indicated which units were woven separately in Figure 8-33.

However, you may prefer to complete each row, picking up the new color as you go along. Try it both ways. Where color changes occur in a vertical line, the yarn is interlooped to avoid a slit (8-32). If a slit is desired as part of your design, or if it is open for only a row or two, start the new color on the next warp thread, without interlooping. Slanting or curving lines do not create slits because the knots go up and step over and no openings are left.

No one color is ever carried over from one design area to another. When a color unit is complete, the end of the weft is cut, even if it was only one knot covering one warp, or if the same color occurs only a few warps over.

As your work progresses, you will notice that the selvages curl under. To correct this, run a piece of yarn through the edge and around the frame every few inches (Figures 8-27, 8-28).

If the direction of the knotting is alternated, the curling will be much less than if the weaving is consistently in one direction. Blocking and pressing will help to flatten the edges of the finished piece.

You will probably find that you are using both hands interchangeably when you work in different directions. Especially on large plain areas with no color change, you can work quite quickly if you hold the weft in your right hand while working left to right and in the left hand coming back the other way. Try it.

Now, finally, you are ready to make the Swedish knot! Remember, you can weave

as much as possible of one color, back and forth in one section of design, until an interloop is necessary. To be correct in doing this technique, there should be not more than three successive knots built up, on the same warp thread without interlooping.

How to make the Swedish knot

The beginning knot is shown in Figure 8-29. Work from the left. Slide your finger under the warp you are going to cover, raising it slightly to help in putting the weft around it. Take the weft yarn under the first warp thread. Bring the cut end over the warp, over the bobbin end of the weft, around through the loop, and pull down on the right side of the warp. This will bring the tail close beside the warp. The bobbin is at the right of the warp ready to start the next stitch.

Note: *The weft always goes over the warp first, then under, up, and down. From right to left, weft is pulled up through, and down to the right of the warp. From left to right, weft is pulled up through and down to the left of the warp.*

The sequence is: weft over the warp, back to left under the same warp, pull straight down. A sharp tug tightens and pulls the knot into place against the row below it. No beating is necessary, because the tightening pull should put it down far enough.

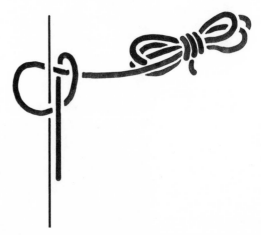

FIGURES 8-29, 30, 31, 32. Methods of making the Swedish knot. 8-29 (above), The beginning knot.

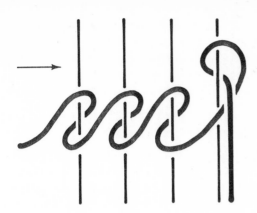

FIGURE 8-30. Left to right.

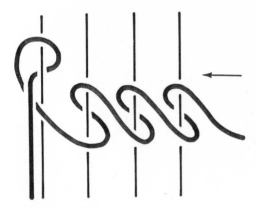

FIGURE 8-31. Right to left.

With practice, you will soon sense just how much to pull in order to make even rows. At first some will be too far apart and some will be a little bumpy, but when you get the idea, good straight rows of ribbing will march along the right side.

Weaving from right to left

This method is exactly the same as weaving from the left, except in reverse (8-31). Notice that when you knot from left to right, the stitches all slant to the right on the working side. When you reverse, all the stitches slant to the left and the fabric will look like knitting or a herringbone pattern on the working side. If you always knot in one direction, all the stitches will slant the same in each row. However, the finished or right side will look exactly the same in every case, regardless of the direction of the work. Figure 8-33 on the next page shows both sides.

When colors interloop

To avoid a slit, interloop colors; make a beginning knot with the new color on the next warp. Tuck the end of the first color down through it and pull the two ends. They will lie parallel to the warp, one at each side (8-32).

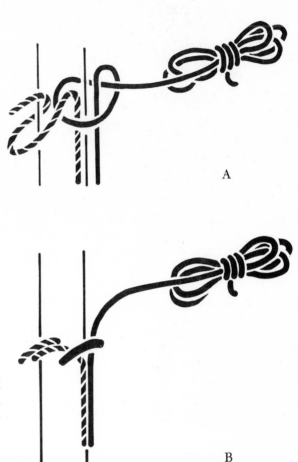

A

B

FIGURE 8-32, A and B. Joining colors to avoid a slit in the weaving.

Continue with the new color until another change is indicated. The new color can be tucked down into the last knot of the first color, if it is more convenient. If a slit is desired, start the new color on the next warp without interlooping into the first color.

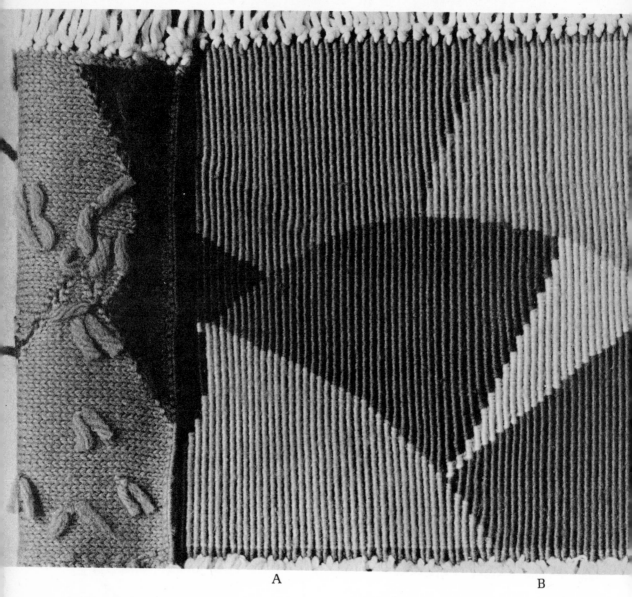

A   B

FIGURE 8-33. Swedish knot tapestry. Note the reverse side folded over; progression of weaving design areas. Unit A can be woven independently. Here unit B was woven independently *after* unit A. (Mrs. V. L. Georgeson, weaver.)

FIGURE 8-34. Hawaiian backstrap loom.

FIGURE 8-35. Close view of interesting textures in the wefts used, combined with several weaving techniques. (Courtesy of Jean J. Williams, weaver. Photograph by Thelma Warner.)

HOW TO WEAVE ON A BACKSTRAP LOOM

A backstrap loom depends upon the weaver for the tightening or loosening of the tension on the warp. One end of the whole warp is fastened to the weaver her-self by means of a strap or belt attached to the cloth beam. The other end of the warp is fastened to a post or hook in the wall. It will seem awkward at first to hitch yourself into such a contrivance, but once you get accustomed to the action you will feel a sense of control not possible with other types of rigid frame looms. (See Chapter 2.)

Weave a sampler

By all means, treat your first attempt as a sampler only. Weave in different weights, colors, and kinds of yarn or dried materials. Try some loops, some soumak, open warp, tied warp, and plain weaving. The hole-and-slot heddle, although rigid, can be freely handled and you can beat the weft in at an angle. Give the backstrap loom a

FIGURE 8-36. Detail of string heddles, weaving sword or batten.

good try and you will find ways to weave that are not possible on fixed looms.

In the past, weaving on backstrap looms was often started at both ends of the loom, working toward the middle. Then, when the space became too narrow for a shuttle or bobbin, the weaving was joined and finished with a needle. This gives a clue to how some old pieces of weaving were accomplished. The joining rows cannot be as perfect as the rest of the weaving because of the difficulty of weaving well in the small space; therefore these rows can be easily identified.

The backstrap loom shown in Figures 8-34 and 2-40, photographed in Hawaii, was warped with lengths of raffia. Linen thread was used for the heddle cord. The tube represents the hollow stick used by primitive weavers to make the second shed. The wefts, exotic and tropical, are raffia and hau fiber in the plain weave areas. Hau fiber is the inner lining of the bark from the hau tree. The heavy brown fiber in the leno (open, lace weave) areas are aerial roots of the banyan tree. The dark, twisted fibers on the surface are branchlets from the royal palm tree (8-35).

How to weave a wall hanging sampler on a backstrap loom

The directions given here are for a loom with looped string heddles. For another way to make and install string heddles see "Heddles" in Chapter 6. For more about backstrap looms with hole-and-slot rigid heddles see Chapter 2.

You will need

Three dowels, each about 12 inches long: two for top and bottom beams, one for heddle stick.

One cardboard tube: the tube from a roll of paper toweling is perfect for making the second shed.

Flat smooth stick or a ruler, for a weaving sword.

Warp: carpet warp, linen, jute, seine twine, raffia.

Weft: your choice. Dried materials, cottons, wools, linens.

Cord for heddles: cotton or linen.

Scissors.

A stationary place to fasten the warp, such as a door knob, a large hook on a wall, a post, or a tree. Look about, and you will find something solid enough. Pick a location with sufficient light and room for a stool or chair — or sit on the ground as primitive weavers do.

How to prepare your warp

One way to wind a continuous warp on a backstrap loom

Fasten one end-dowel to the edge of a table with a C-clamp, so that most of the dowel projects beyond the table edge. Place the other end-dowel 36 inches from the first one, in a similar position. Tie one end of the warp thread an inch or so in from the end, around the dowel. Wind it back and forth between dowels, around and around, 33 times. You now have a warp of 33 threads, 36 inches long, already wound on the top and bottom beams of your loom.

Spread the warp threads slightly apart on each dowel, so your warp is about 5 inches wide, making sure that the threads are straight and in order. Weave in two rows for a binder thread, using a length of warp thread. Press this in close to the dowel. Weave over and under, then return. Beat in. Repeat this procedure at the other end.

How to put in the heddles

While the warp is still held taut, put in the string heddles. Tie one end of the heddle cord to the heddle stick (dowel). Hold the heddle stick above the warp with one hand, and with the other, carry the heddle cord down under the second warp thread, back up and around the heddle stick, down under the fourth warp thread, back up and around the heddle stick, and so on, picking up every other warp. These will all be raised up when the heddle stick is lifted, to make one shed for the weft to go through. Keep the loops about $1\frac{1}{2}$ inches long, and as even as you can.

After the last heddle is looped, cut the

FIGURE 8-37. String heddle shed open.

FIGURE 8-38. The second shed, held open by the tube. Shows position of heddle rod when not in use. Weaving sword is about to beat the weft in. (Courtesy of Jean J. Williams, weaver. Photograph by Thelma Warner.)

heddle cord and tie to the heddle stick (8-37). Pick up the alternate warp threads with the tube to make the second shed (8-38). A cord is run through and tied at the top of the tube for a lifter.

Tie a length of cord to each end of the warp dowel, to loop or tie around the doorknob, hook, or whatever you are using to suspend the loom. Release the loom from the C clamp, being careful not to tangle it, and hang up.

How to get into the loom

Before you tie the loom around your waist be sure that all of your weaving materials are within reach! Fasten a strip of cloth or soft cord to one end of the waist dowel. Take this strip around your back, and tie it at the other end of the dowel.

Now you are ready to weave

Weave in a few rows of plain weave, over and under, beating in to the binder thread, for a heading or hem. Then start your sampling, with whatever weft and technique you choose. When you have woven as far as you can reach, untie one end of the strap around your back and roll the finished weaving around the waist dowel. Put the strap around your waist again, retie it to the loose end of the waist dowel, and continue weaving. Finish with another several rows of plain weaving for a heading or hem.

When the weaving is finished, cut the warp at the end near the warp beam, pull the warps out of the heddle loops and finish the warp ends however you wish. They can be knotted, braided, trimmed, and turned back in a hem.

If you prefer, you can cut the string heddles off, remove everything but the two end dowels, and use the warp dowel as the hanger.

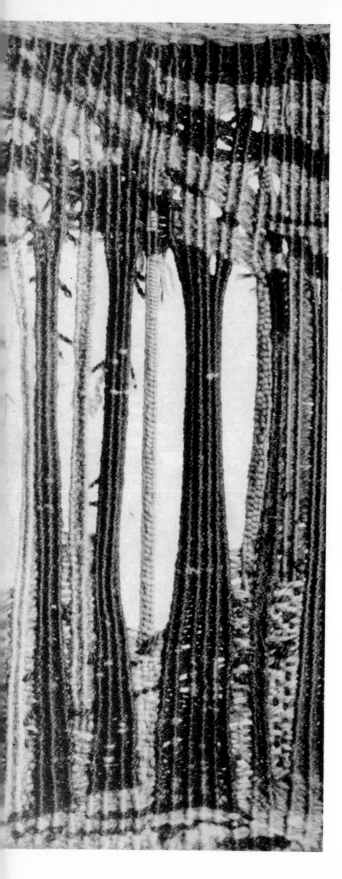

Planning, preparing, gathering, and weaving material for this book has been such a great pleasure for me that I hope some measure of my enthusiasm and respect for the weaving craft comes through to you. Weaving, stitchery, anything to do with textiles, has always been of endless interest to me and I know there will never be enough time to try, read about, and see all of the techniques.

Perhaps you, too, will be started on a new interest through this book. Perhaps experienced weavers will be inspired to follow a trail new to them. My sincere wish is that all of you who want to try this very old craft, with its exciting new approaches and adaptations, will find a point of departure and a lift along the way in *Weaving is for Anyone.*

Jean Wilson

BIBLIOGRAPHY

The following are just a very few of the many books available that are of interest and help to weavers. Look in your public libraries, book stores, and consult your craft-book lists. There are any number of small books and booklets about special, regional weaving. Keep looking, and you will find some happy surprises to give you ideas for your weaving.

Design

Albers, Anni, *On Designing*, Pellango Press, New Haven, Connecticut, 1959.

Appleton, Leroy H., *Indian Art of the Americas*, Charles Scribner's Sons, New York, 1950.

Bager, Bertel, *Nature as Designer*, Reinhold Publishing Corporation, New York, 1966.

Ballinger/Vroman, *Design—Sources and Resources*, Reinhold Publishing Corporation, New York, 1966.

Enciso, Jorge, *Design Motifs of Ancient Mexico*, Dover Publications, Inc., New York, 1953.

Hartung, Rolf, *More Creative Textile Design*, Reinhold Publishing Corporation, New York, 1965.

Inverarity, Robert Bruce, *Art of the Northwest Coast Indians*, University of California, Berkeley, 1950.

Laliberte/McIlhany, *Banners and· Hangings*, Reinhold Publishing Corporation, New York, 1966.

Miles, Walter, *Designs for Craftsmen*, Doubleday & Company, Inc., New York, 1962.

Additional Design Sources: catalogs of crafts exhibits, museum catalogs, regional booklets, brochures, periodicals (*American Fabrics, Ciba Review, Craft Horizons, Handweaver & Craftsman, School Arts, Arizona Highways, Country Beautiful, National Geographic*), and The Sierra Club Book Series.

General Crafts

Griswold, Lester, *Handicraft Simplified: Procedure and Projects*, Outwest Printing and Stationery Company, Colorado Springs, 1942.

Harvey, Virginia Isham, *Macramé: The Art of Creative Knotting*, Reinhold Publishing Corporation, New York, 1967.

Johnson, Pauline, Hazel Koenig, and Spencer Moseley, *Crafts Design*, Wadsworth Publishing Corporation, Inc., Belmont, California, 1962.

Newkirk, Lewis V., *Integrated Handwork for Elementary Schools*, Silver Burdette Company, New York-Boston-Chicago-Sante Fe, 1940.

Stitchery

Enthoven, Jacqueline, *The Stitches of Creative Embroidery*, Reinhold Publishing Corporation, New York, 1964.

Krevitzky, Nik, *Stitchery: Art and Craft*, Reinhold Publishing Corporation, New York, 1966.

Stenton, Sir Frank, ed., *Bayeux Tapestry*, Phaidon Art Books, New York, 1965.

Van Dommelen, David B., *Decorative Wall Hangings: Art with Fabric*, Funk & Wagnalls Company, New York, 1962.

Tapestry

Candee, Helen Churchill, *The Tapestry Book*, Frederick A. Stokes Company, New York, 1912.

Fischer, Ernst, and Gertrud Ingers, *Framskvavnad (Flemish Weaving)*, Landby and Lundgrens, Boktryckeri, Malmö, Sweden, 1961.

Kybal, Antonin, *Modern Textile Designs*, (English text), Jan Spurny, Artia, Czechoslovakia, 1960.

Sevensma, W. S., *Tapestries*, Universe Books, Inc., New York, 1965.

Tidball, Harriett, *Contemporary Tapestry*, Shuttle Craft Monograph Twelve, Craft & Hobby Book Service, Big Sur, California, 1964.

Weaving, Textiles

Allard, Mary, *Rug Making: Techniques and Design*, Chilton Company, Philadelphia-New York, 1963.

Baity, Elizabeth Chesley, *Man Is a Weaver*, Viking Press, Inc., New York, 1942.

Birrell, Verla, *The Textile Arts: A Handbook of Fabric Structure and Design Processes*, Harper and Row, New York, 1959.

Black, Mary E., *New Key to Weaving*, The Bruce Publishing Company, Milwaukee, 1957.

D'Harcourt, Raoul, *Textiles of Ancient Peru and Their Techniques*, trans. by Sadie Brown; Grace G. Denny and Carolyn Osborn, eds., University of Washington Press, Seattle, 1962.

Greer, Gertrude, *Adventures in Weaving*, Charles A. Bennett Company, Inc., Peoria, Illinois, 1951.

Hooper, *Hand Loom Weaving*, Pitman Publishing Corporation, New York and Chicago, 1920.

Kent, Kate Peck, *Story of Navajo Weaving*, McGrew Printing & Lithographing Company, Phoenix, Arizona, 1961.

O'Neale, Lila M., *Textiles of Highland Guatamala* (Publication #567), Carnegie Institution of Washington, D.C., 1945.

Roth, Ling H., *Studies in Primitive Looms*, F. King and Sons, Halifax, Nova Scotia, 1934.

Tovey, John, *The Technique of Weaving*, Reinhold Publishing Corporation, New York, 1965.

INDEX